Getting to Grips with God

Thanks to Jane for her love
and no-nonsense advice

To Tim Snowdon
for the photo on the back

And to all the following
for inspirational ideas
and week-by-week work

Jane Blazeby
Jo Frost
Pete Halestrap
George Harker
John Lawrie
Clare Mason
Al Massey
Jane Norman
Sarah Rooper
Sarah Steel
Anna Williams

**The voice of the Lord strikes
with flashes of lightning**

Psalm 29:7 (NIV)

GETTING TO GRIPS WITH GOD

NICK JONES

The Bible Reading Fellowship
OPENING THE BIBLE

Text and illustrations copyright © 1996 Nick Jones

Published by
The Bible Reading Fellowship
Peter's Way, Sandy Lane West
Oxford, England
ISBN 0 7459 3254 1
Albatross Books Pty Ltd
PO Box 320, Sutherland
NSW 2232, Australia
ISBN 0 7324 0942 X

First edition 1996
10 9 8 7 6 5 4 3 2 1 0

Acknowledgments
Unless otherwise stated, scripture is quoted from
the **Good News Bible**, published by The Bible
Societies/HarperCollins Publishers Ltd., UK, ©
American Bible Society, 1966, 1971, 1976, 1992

The Holy Bible, New International Version (NIV), ©
1973, 1978, 1984 by International Bible Society. Used
by permission.

Cover photograph: Zefa UK

A catalogue record for this book is available
from the British Library

Printed and bound in Malta

Contents

Letter to leaders

Getting to Grips with God was originally written because we wished to offer the young people in our youth group the opportunity to grapple with the absolute basics of the Christian faith. We wanted them to be able to investigate the claims of Christianity in an open and friendly environment where they could ask those nagging questions that may (or may not) have kept them awake at night. Questions such as: Does God exist? Why am I alive? What has gone wrong with the world? To this end we ran the course as an extra series of meetings held in our home and open to anyone who wanted to find out more. *Getting to Grips with God* is ideally suited to that kind of group, but it is perfectly appropriate to run it with young people of varying levels of interest and commitment.

Getting to Grips with God was also written in answer to a concern I have that we adult Christians often assume that our young people understand more about the Christian faith than they really do. Children do have real spiritual insight, but they need the opportunity to get to grips with the basics. Unless you get the basics straight, the Christian faith can become little more than a restricting set of do's and don'ts. If, for example, we don't appreciate God's mind-boggling love for us, then the prospect of having to love other people can seem nothing but drudgery. When, on the other hand, we are overwhelmed by God's love for us, loving others becomes a natural response.

Going back to basics is a valuable experience for us all, leaders and young people alike. It enables us to focus on the key truths of the Christian faith and refresh ourselves as to their astonishing implications. It is also a great joy and privilege to see young people grappling with the truth and coming to meet God for themselves.

Getting to Grips with God is made up of ten meetings. The first five investigate the essential questions of God's existence, the meaning of life, the person of Jesus, the point of the cross, and conclude by offering the young people the opportunity to become Christians. The second five meetings investigate what being a Christian is all about and are based on Jesus' instruction to 'Love God with all your heart, soul and mind, and love your neighbour as yourself.' This is tackled through meetings on prayer, the Bible, the Holy Spirit, God's family and the power of love.

My hope and prayer for this course is that it would enable both you and your group to get to grips with God and that he in turn would get to grips with you.

Striking Out

The following hints will explain to you
What youthwork's about and what leaders should do.

I decided to follow Jesus as a teenager, as did my wife Jane. According to a recent report commissioned by the General Synod of the Church of England, sixty-five per cent of adult Christians took 'significant steps towards faith before the age of thirteen'.[2] We, like the majority of Christians, are living proof that youthwork can have a lifelong impact, and are both immensely grateful to those people who patiently sowed and watered the seeds of faith in our lives. With the enormous range of influences on young people today it is particularly important that we provide good youth groups where young people can investigate and meet God for themselves.

It was as very inexperienced youth leaders, aged twenty-five and twenty-three, that Jane and I agreed to take on the running of our church's group for eleven to fourteen-year-olds. Not surprisingly we made, and have continued to make, many mistakes in the six years since. The following hints on leading a youth group are a distillation of the lessons we have learnt. We hope that they will save you and your group some of the pain that comes from learning by trial and error and will equip you to do the job well.

Using me?

Whether you are considering youth work from a distance or are in it up to your neck, I would like you to spend a little time thinking about the following two questions.

● Is your relationship with God alive and growing?

● Do you like young people and want to help them to meet God?

I believe that these are vital qualities in a youthworker and that your answer should really be 'yes' to each question. A love for God is 'caught not taught' so it is important that you as a leader are in love with God and dependent on his Holy Spirit. Don't be daunted by this, but try to walk closely with God and in your busyness make sure you don't neglect your own need for fellowship and teaching.

Hint one: love

The most important thing that you can do for any young person is to show them God's love by caring about them. This is the most powerful visual aid in youthwork. You don't need to be young and attractive with your finger on the pulse of contemporary youth culture to be a good youth leader. What your group members want to know is whether you care about them, whether you like them and are interested in them. One of the most effective leaders we have ever had in our team was a wonderful silver-haired and godly lady in her fifties. The young people in our group loved her because they instinctively knew that she cared about them and was interested in the things that made up their lives; they could talk to her about anything.

Of course good teaching is important, but in the balance of influences it is easily outweighed by the influence of practical love. To demonstrate this, try listing six sermons, talks or meetings that have played a significant part in your growth as a Christian. Then list six people who have played a key role in your Christian life. I am sure that the second list will more easily come to mind. The most effective way in which we communicate the truths and reality of the Christian faith is not the way we teach them, but the way we live. If our young people feel that we respect, accept and care about them and if they can see that our relationship with God is real they will begin to believe that God is real too. So get to know your group members and let them get to know you. Arrange outings, take them to the swimming pool or invite them round to your home for a pizza and video.

As the group gets to know you, they will observe all that goes on, and particularly the way in which the leaders relate to each other. Christian love and friendship should be seen in the leadership team. The other day we asked our young people to complete a questionnaire about the group. One of the questions asked what they would remember about the group in seventy years' time. We were touched by the response of one person who replied, 'the laughing leaders'.

Hint two: prayer

Prayer is a vital part of youthwork. Surround all your work and planning with prayer. Pray for the young people in your group. Pray for any other leaders in your team. Pray with the other leaders in your team. Put them all on a prayer rota so that you pray for them weekly. Beyond that seek out a number of people in the church who will commit themselves to praying for your group and its leaders. Keep them regularly informed about what to pray for either in a prayer letter or over the phone. Get your prayer requests printed in the church prayer diary or on its service sheet.

Hint three: teaching

Jesus was an outstanding teacher—enthusiastic, clear and inspiring. I often wonder how we can become like that. Think back to your school days. What made the good teachers stand out from the rest? I was inspired by the teachers who knew and loved their subject and had a real desire to help their students understand and enjoy it. Invariably they made every effort to bring their subject to life and were prepared to spend extra time helping their students get to grips with it.

If your group sense that you love God, are excited by following Jesus and really want them to discover God's love for themselves, then you are already more than half-way there.

The next chapter deals with the practicalities of 'how' to teach well and all the 'Lightning Bolts' material has been designed to help you explore the Bible and the Christian faith with your group in a relevant, positive and exciting way.

Well, actually Vicar it's not going too well!

Hint four: church backing

Youthwork is a key part of the work of the wider church. So make sure that the leaders of your church know what you are up to and are behind you in your aims and objectives. They should take an interest in what you are doing and support you. However, it may be more practical for them to nominate a senior member of the church to oversee what you are doing and to whom you are accountable. This person should be concerned for your spiritual growth and personal welfare just as you are concerned for the spiritual growth and personal needs of your leaders and young people. Meet with them regularly, pray together and keep them informed about how it's going. If your church is unable to arrange this for you ask a friend to support you or get your fellowship or house group to do it.

Hint five: building up a leadership team

Any group with more than ten members will probably need more than one leader. We find that the ideal leader—group-member ratio is roughly one to six, preferably matched sex to sex. We have found working with other leaders and managing our team one of the most rewarding and enjoyable parts of youthwork. As overall leader your main responsibility is to the other members of your team. Care for them, train them, teach them, set them a good example. Perhaps you could eat a meal together once a month when you plan and pray for the group. Keep in touch with how things are going with each of them at home, at work and with God. Be sensitive to the other pressures on your leaders; lighten their load when they have exams or increased pressure at work or home. Do let them know that you appreciate them; perhaps send them a postcard from your holidays or a small present at Christmas and don't forget to say 'thank you' regularly. A happy leadership team leads to a happy youth group.

We have given the whole process of enlisting new leaders a great deal of thought. This is our method. Start by praying, and sending out some prayer requests to anyone who prays for your group. Ask your leaders to see if they have any friends who might be interested or see if there is anyone you know. Potentially this is a very fruitful avenue to pursue; most of our leaders past and present have come through this route. Ask the church leaders if they know of anyone who might be suitable. Possibly give out a request for help in a church service explaining what is needed and what is involved. You may be surprised by some of the people that turn up, but if they have the following qualities they most definitely have the potential to become a good youth leader:

● a living relationship with God

● an ability to get on with young people

● enthusiasm, willingness to learn and enough time

Arrange a time to chat with or 'interview' any potential candidates. You need to know about their experience, suitability, compatibility with the present team, their aims and ambitions, weaknesses and background. Consider asking for a reference. Remember that your responsibility is to the young people in your care. This 'interview' equally gives the potential leader the chance to find out about you and the job. Pray together and if appropriate offer them a trial period of say four weeks. This is a good opportunity for you both to take a more in-depth look at each other and the group. Do make it clear that both sides can say 'no' at the end of the four weeks. We have had very few leaders with whom the feelings haven't been mutual.

Assuming that you both decide that they should join the team ask them to commit themselves to the work for a minimum period of time, perhaps a year. Make it clear that they can always come and ask if they are not sure about anything or are having problems. Keep a friendly eye on them and perhaps regularly meet up and review how things are going. Don't drop them in the deep end, but let them gradually gain experience at leading groups and doing things 'up front'. Remember to give them plenty of encouragement and positive feedback.

Hint six: the right environment

Make every effort to think of ways of making your meeting room more friendly. Think about the seating arrangements—chairs, floor or mats? Think about the wall and ceiling space and whether you could use them for visual aids. Think about the temperature, lighting and privacy. Consider whether it is worth trying to change rooms. Providing a comfortable environment will make the world of difference. Perhaps you could get your group involved in transforming your room. Over the years we have accumulated all sorts of visual aids and junk which we have lying around most of the time. This makes the room a bit like a treasure trove and the young people absorb important information just by being there.

If you live near the church and have a small group perhaps you could try meeting in your home. The young people are guaranteed to enjoy it.

Hint seven: parents

Getting to know the parents of your group members will help you understand their family background. It also enables the parents to get to know you and have the confidence to entrust their children into your care. They will only do this if they feel sure that you are responsible and competent. So be courteous and friendly and keep them informed about what is going on with programme cards, notes on outing times and dates, and plenty of advance warning. Always be meticulous about all aspects of safety and hygiene. Communicating with parents who are not Christians is particularly important as they may be concerned about their child's involvement with the church.

Hint eight: a clear aim

The reason for having an aim for your group is to achieve it. Without an aim you risk achieving nothing. The aim of our group is that every member has a positive and enjoyable encounter with the Christian faith. Our leaders know this and whenever we lose our way we come back to it. So decide on a sentence that sums up the reason for your group's existence. It will be an invaluable help as you make decisions about all aspects of the group's life.

It is also helpful to set yourself short-term objectives. For example, if you are just starting out you might set yourself the objective of establishing a regular group within six months. The leaders of a growing group might set themselves the objective of building up a leadership team or getting their group members reading the Bible at home.

In conclusion

Young people matter to God. They are his children and he longs for them to come to know him, but he needs people like you to introduce him to them and help them to grow. If you are willing, God will use you in some very exciting ways, some of which you will never have even imagined. At times it will be tough, and you will frequently be disappointed, but don't give up. You are doing a vital job that is treasured by God.

Nick and Jane

Running a meeting

Running a meeting, large, medium or small:
The following tips apply to them all.

Your week-by-week meetings are a fantastic window of opportunity through which God can touch the lives of your group members, so make the most of the time. The members of your group will probably spend the 168 hours of their week something like this: 65 hours asleep, 40 hours at school, 35 hours at home, 12 hours of television, 10 hours with friends, 5 hours eating, but only 1 hour at your youth group. That hour or so may even be the only contact some of the members of your group have with the Christian faith.

The following ten tips will help you to lead your meetings well and so maximize their impact. They all apply whether you are leading a small discussion group or a larger group meeting.

Members of larger youth groups will benefit from the opportunity to spend part of each week's meeting in smaller cells. Do arrange this if at all possible. This is often where the real work is done. In small groups your young people can explore and chat through the subject, pray together and get to know each other and their leader. The other advantage of regular small groups is that each leader is identified with a handful of young people for whom they can pray and have a special concern.

The first five tips are concerned with preparation for the meeting, and the second five with personal 'on the day' leadership skills.

Tip one: plan ahead

Start planning the next meeting well before it happens. Meet with the other members of the team the week before and plan and pray together. Make sure that you are all clear about the aim for the meeting and discuss exactly what will be taught so that you are all saying the same thing. Arrange who will lead the main part, who is going to do what, and whose responsibility it is to get props and equipment together.

Tip two: pray

Prayer is a vital part of your preparation. Spend time praying both on your own and with the other leaders. Pray for the meeting: that God would use all that you have planned. Pray for the other leaders and the parts they will be playing. Pray for the group members, preferably by name: that God would speak to them through what you do.

Tip three: know your subject

Make sure that you understand the essential facts about your subject, or the plot of the story that you are teaching, and know how to explain them simply. You don't have to have a thorough grasp of the varying branches of theological insight on the topic, but you do need to understand the basics and what they mean to you, whether it be the Holy Spirit, Balaam's ass, or prayer.

Tip four: be ready

On the day arrive early and allow plenty of time to get everything organized and ready well before your group arrives. Run through any sketches, talks and the general plan for the meeting before the group descend upon you. Make sure that you have all the equipment you need—Bibles, pens, paper—and that you know where you have put them. Spend the limited time you have with your group members concentrating on them and not trying to find the sonic infra-red X-ray specs that you need for the Bible reading.

Tip five: get the group involved

We all learn best by 'doing'. All of us remember far more of what we 'do' than what we just 'hear' or 'see'. So get the young people involved in the meeting wherever possible, with readings, sketches, music or artwork; anything that they would enjoy, even just helping to set up the room.

Tip six: create a relaxed atmosphere

Creating a relaxed atmosphere in your group takes time. The key is to be relaxed yourself: it's contagious. Start by standing near the door and individually welcoming the group members by name and with a big smile as they arrive. Have some other leaders milling around to chat to the group and particularly any new people. The first time I went to a youth group I left within three minutes because no one spoke to me. I tried again a few weeks later and to my astonishment was greeted by a friendly face who even knew my name; after that I never looked back. Make every effort to get to know each person's name and use it. This is a very practical way of showing that you care and, as I found out, makes the world of difference.

Seating arrangements are also an important part of creating a relaxed atmosphere. In a large meeting encourage everyone to sit closely together, rather than spread out round the room. In small discussion groups get everyone sitting in a circle so they can all see each other. Don't let little clusters sit in opposite corners or behind each other. Use comfy chairs if possible, or sit on the floor, perhaps on mats.

An important way of creating a relaxed atmosphere in small groups is to let the group chat with each other. Start your small group times by asking how their week has been and what they have been up to. Remember that the young people will be more shy than you so it's up to you to take the initiative in conversation and in directing the meeting. Let the quiet and shy individuals stay quiet; if you don't put pressure on them they will, in time, come out of themselves and get more involved in the group.

Tip seven: learn to listen

An essential part of leading a small group is listening to the group members. This comes naturally to some, but we can all learn to do it better. Learn to listen to snippets of conversation and throw-away remarks and, when appropriate, pick up on these either at the time or later. They can tell you about what is going on in a young person's life and can sometimes be tentative requests for help. During activities listen thoughtfully to the group members' comments about what you are doing and never interrupt them. Always focus your full attention on the person to whom you are talking.

Tip eight: be enthusiastic

Enthusiasm is infectious and will soon spread among the members of your group. Be enthusiastic about the activities you are doing and don't plan anything for the group that you don't find interesting and can't be enthusiastic about.

Tip nine: a note on discipline

In theory, if you are well-prepared and give your group a stimulating and action-packed programme they won't have either the time or inclination to muck around. Trouble is likely to arise if the young people are bored or not interested. However, the group can be hard to handle when, through no fault of your own, they are gripped by a collective 'bad mood' or reckless over-excitability. Personally I would rather have a noisy group who are obviously enjoying themselves and involved in what we are doing than a 'well-behaved' group who just sit there in silence. However, you may also have the odd individual who seems determined to disrupt your meeting despite your best efforts. Don't let them spoil the meeting for the rest of the group. Here are some suggestions to help you deal with any situations like this:

● Get another leader to sit by the child throughout the meeting. Their very presence should be a restraining influence, but they could also pray for the child and where necessary have a word in their ear.

● Have a quiet 'man to man' or 'woman to woman' type conversation with the young person afterwards. Find out how they feel about the meetings and try to get them on your side.

● Try to get them involved in the meeting. Perhaps they could take part in a sketch, or preparing some visual aids, anything that will help to make them feel valued and perhaps a little more responsible.

It is often true that a young person who is 'causing trouble' in the group is particularly in need of your love and encouragement. Try to see this as an opportunity, not a problem.

Susan, when you've finished tying up the boys could you tell us what we learnt last week...

Tip ten: take stock

Naturally, and for a variety of reasons, some meetings will go better than others so don't be discouraged if you seem to be taking a while to learn the art of leading a meeting (it took us years and we're still learning). At the end of each meeting try and work out whether you achieved your aim for the meeting. Ask yourself why it was that you did or didn't succeed. Try and put what you learn into practice next time. When things don't go quite as you hoped, talk to God about it and ask for his help. Chat with your other leaders and perhaps a member of the church leadership. Above all, keep going because, whether you realize it or not, God will still be at work drawing the young people to himself.

Nick and Jane

How to use 'Lightning Bolts'

A quick tour round the layout of this book,
The what, why and how—and where you should look.

There are two elements to each title in 'Lightning Bolts': the leaders' guides and the daily Bible reading notes. They both explore the same theme or book from the Bible and can be used together or apart. The leaders' guides provide you with ten complete meeting plans full of clear ideas of ways to communicate and unpack the message of the Bible with both small and large groups. Each meeting plan contains the following elements:

Leaders' information

The aim

A clearly expressed aim for the meeting.

The lightning bolt

The Bible passage on which the meeting is based.

Equipment checklist

A list of equipment needed for the meeting.

Letter to leaders

A personal introduction to the subject of the meeting along with one or two thought-provoking questions to help you apply it to your life.

Ideas for the meeting

Each of the different ideas or activities suggested for each meeting falls into one of the following eight categories and will always be identified by its symbol. The first four are 'presentations' to the group and are usually suggested for use when your group is all together. The second four are 'activities' for the group members and so are more suitable for smaller discussion groups, though some of them could be used with larger groups. They are, however, all loosely interchangeable so that you can pick and mix in the light of your group's needs and the amount of space and time that you have available.

Presentations

 Sparking off

Presentations that introduce and set the scene for the meeting.

 The main bolt

The Bible passage presented or experienced.

 Shock waves

Presentations exploring the implications of 'The main bolt' and how it is relevant today.

 In a flash

The main point of the meeting summed up in a flash.

Activities

 Charging up

Ice-breaker activities to get the group members charged up and ready.

 Explosions

Activities in which the group members explore and unpack the Bible passage together.

 Striking home

Activities that help the group take the point of the meeting on board and, if appropriate, apply it to their lives.

 **Return strikes**

An opportunity for the group to pray together.

Getting to Grips with God
Special features

Headline questions

Play the *Getting to Grips with God* theme music as the group arrives (on the *Getting to Grips with God* cassette, see page 143). Kick off each meeting with an outline of the kind of questions with which you will be grappling in the session. Dress one of your leaders or members up as 'Question Mark'—a newspaper-seller type wearing raincoat, scarf and hat marked with a '?'. After you have welcomed the group and introduced the subject of the meeting Question Mark wanders in and shouts out five headline questions. Thank Mark for his questions and move on to the next presentation.

Smash 'n' Grab

**Getting the
point
2 mins**

The Smash 'n' Grab feature consists of two hands in conversation. Each week Smash explains and sums up the point of the meeting to Grab who finally gets it.

To run this feature you need to make a small screen with a tissue paper window. This is cheap and fairly easy to make. Full instructions are on pages 20 and 21. If you haven't got time or are not too good at DIY why not ask a friend or member of the church to do it for you.

Back-light the screen with an angle poised lamp so that you can make hand silhouettes on the tissue paper. In front of the tissue paper is a small ledge on which sits a tennis ball otherwise known as 'the point'. Once Grab has got the point he smashes through the tissue paper screen and grabs 'the point'.

Some tips
- *Put the Smash 'n' Grab stand on a table and open out the arms with the hanging fabric. Spot light the tissue paper screen from behind with a 100W angle poised lamp about 18 inches back.*
- *When 'performing' Smash 'n' Grab two leaders stand either side of the screen behind the hanging fabric. Make your hand gestures clear and dramatic. There are lots of expressive gestures you could use: Thumbs up, thumb and first finger making an 'O' shape, pointing, waving, hand open palm up, etc.*
- *Keep a close eye on the shadows on the screen. What you see is what the group see. The closer your hands are to the screen the clearer the shadow will be.*
- *Aim high when you smash through the screen and you are more likely to get the point!*
- *Before the next meeting rip off all the tissue paper, smear glue all round the front edge of the window and stretch a fresh piece of tissue paper across.*

Making a Smash 'n' Grab Screen

Equipment Required

A.	Two 110cm lengths of 25 x 50mm timber	Uprights
B.	Three 75cm lengths of 25 x 50mm timber	Cross pieces
C.	Two 50cm lengths of 25 x 50mm timber	Feet
D.	One 25cm length of 25 x 50mm timber	Platform
E.	10cm length of thick cardboard tubing about 5cm wide	Platform
F.	62 x 75cm hardboard	Front
G.	Two hardboard triangles 40 x 30 x 30cm	Supports
H.	Two 75cm lengths of baton	Arms
I.	Two 75 x 185cm lengths of cheap fabric (calico)	Curtains
J.	Ten 50 x 75cm sheets of white tissue Paper	Screen
K.	Red cardboard triangle labelled 'THE POINT' 12 x 12 x 12cm	Pointer
L.	Tennis Ball	The point

4 cm screws or nails, washers, wood glue & tacks

Before you start ring up your local art materials shop and find out what size tissue paper they sell. The dimensions of this screen are for tissue paper 50 x 75cm. If you can't get tissue paper this size adapt the the screen to fit the tissue paper you can buy. **The window must be at least five cm smaller all round than the tissue paper.**

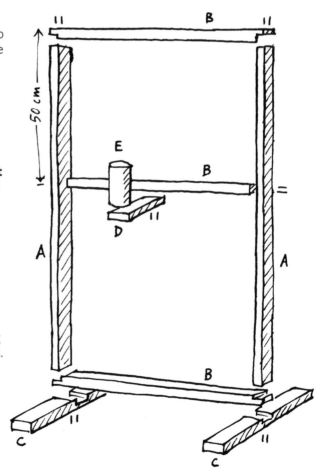

Step One

Assemble the lengths of 25 x 50mm timber as shown in this diagram using wood glue and screws/nails. Glue the card-board tube to the platform with wood glue and a nail or two.

Step Two

Attach the hardboard front and support triangles using glue and tacks. Staple fabric to the baton arms and screw these to the top of the screen, so that they can fold back.

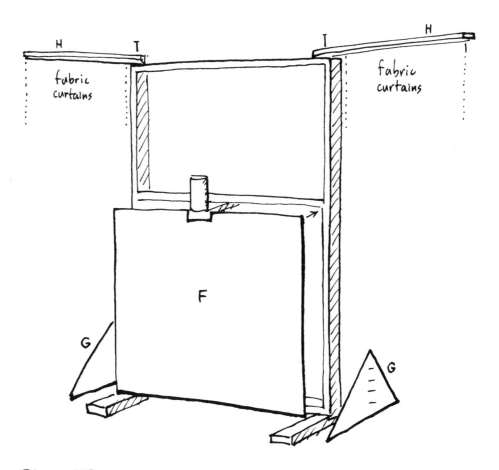

Step Three

Give the whole thing a lick of paint (white), smear wood glue round the window and stretch a piece of tissue paper across the front. Attach a triangle of cardboard labelled 'The Point' to the front end of the platform. Write Smash 'n' Grab across the front of the screen.

The Hot Seat

Interrogation time
4 mins

The Hot Seat is a regular feature in which the group members get the opportunity to ask one of the leaders questions about their understanding and experience of the topic of the meeting. All you need is a chair, an angle poised lamp and the Hot Seat theme music on the audio cassette (see page 143). Turn out the lights, point the lamp at the chair and play the music. Ask the selected leader to take a seat and explain to the group that they can ask anything they like about his or her experience of God, prayer or whatever you're grappling with in the meeting. This always proved very popular with our group, but you might need to set the ball rolling by asking some juicy questions of your own.

The key to making the Hot Seat feature work well is creating a relaxed atmosphere where the young people feel safe about asking questions. Always advise the inhabitant of the Hot Seat to keep their answers SHORT and above all HONEST. It does not matter if they can't answer a question. It is fine to simply say that you don't know the answer. After all the leaders in your group have had their week on the Hot Seat why not invite some special guests in to be grilled by the group? Perhaps you could invite your vicar or minister, an older member of the teenage youth group or perhaps even a parent.

The questions box

Qs & As
2 mins

An important part of *Getting to Grips with God* is giving the group members the opportunity to ask questions about the Christian faith. To encourage this have a questions box (shoe box with a slit in the top) in the room into which they can slip their questions. Explain that questions put in the box will be answered in one of the following meetings. If the questioner would rather have a personal answer they should sign their name on their question slip and one of the leaders will discuss their question with them individually.

At the end of the book are outline answers to ten commonly asked questions about the Christian faith. Also listed are twenty questions that are dealt with in *Getting to Grips with God* meetings. If any of these questions are asked, I suggest you explain that they will be dealt with later in the course. When answering questions it is best to keep your replies short and honest. Many issues raised will not have simple easy answers so it is best to acknowledge this rather than over-simplify.

Worksheets

Each *Getting to Grips with God* meeting outline comes with a worksheet. Master copies of these on pages 123–142. Please photocopy-enlarge these (at 141%) onto both sides of A4 sheets. Copy enough for your group members and fold each twice along the dotted lines to make a tall, slim leaflet. It is quite possible to run *Getting to Grips with God* without the worksheets but they do add an extra dimension to the meeting as well as providing the group members with something to take home.

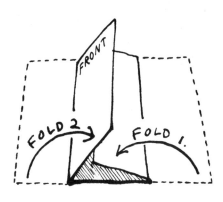

Planning your meeting

Each 'Lightning Bolts' meeting plan contains a selection of activities and ideas for you to take and adapt in the light of your own group's needs. Here are some suggestions on how to plan each meeting.

● Read through the leaders' information and all the material.

● Make sure that you are clear about your aim.

● Select only those suggestions and activities that are appropriate for your leaders and group.

● Add your own ideas and worship to create your own style of meeting. Each 'Lightning Bolts' meeting plan is a starting point on which you can build. Please feel free to adapt it as much as is necessary.

Daily readings

Each of the titles in 'Lightning Bolts' is accompanied by ten weeks of daily Bible readings for eleven to fourteen-year-olds. These take the reader all the way through the appropriate book of the Bible or explore selected Bible passages using an amusing and hands-on approach to strike home their message. Do encourage your group members to use them. They will help them get stuck into Bible reading and reinforce all that you are doing in your weekly meetings.

Audio cassette

An audio cassette is available to accompany *Getting to Grips with God*. It contains all the sound effects and theme tunes which you need to run this course. See page 143 for details.

Photocopiable material

The following material from *Getting to Grips with God* can be photocopied for use with your group:

● The ten worksheets (see above) on pages 123–142

● The instructions for making a Smash 'n' Grab screen on pages 20–21

● The six illustrations for The Rt Hon. Richard Hindley Watson Grouch MP story on pages 98–103. These can be photocopied onto acetates for use with an overhead projector.

● The 'What is God like?' cards on page 32.

● The Problem Page letters on page 66.

1

Getting to Grips
with God

The Aim: To consider the evidence for God's existence and find out a little about him.

The Lightning Bolt: Romans 1:20.
Creation points to God's existence.

Equipment Checklist:

PRESENTATIONS
- ❏ theme music on tape
- ❏ Question Mark outfit
- ❏ hats for quotes
- ❏ multi-sensory experience bits
- ❏ Hot Seat, light & music
- ❏ questions box
- ❏ Smash 'n' Grab kit

ACTIVITIES
- ❏ worksheets & pens
- ❏ photos of nature
- ❏ copies of God word cards
- ❏ copies of daily readings

Letter to leaders

The million dollar question 'Does God exist?' is perhaps not so crucial as we might at first think. This is because the majority of people worldwide have an inexplicable hunch that he does (and in any case it's impossible to prove his existence one way or the other). What is much more important therefore is the question, 'What is God like?'

The natural tendency is to think of God in terms of perfected human characteristics: love, goodness and justice, etc. Such a God is little more than a cosmic human being; a God created in our own image. This, however, is not accurate because the Bible clearly tells us that many of God's qualities have absolutely no parallel in human experience; he is eternal, he depends on nothing else, he is utterly consistent, he is infinite and all-powerful, he is present everywhere and knows and sees everything. The Old and New Testaments give us glimpses of an utterly awesome God, an extraordinary unity of personal love and unlimited power, of majesty and gentleness. A God far beyond human imagining, but one who passionately loves each one of us and wants us to know and love him.

- *Why is it that you believe or know that God exists?*

- *How would you begin to describe God to someone who had never heard of him before?*

Presentations

Headline questions

**Welcome &
introduction**
2 mins

Try and create a warm, friendly atmosphere and have the *Getting to Grips with God* theme music playing as the group arrives (on audio cassette, see page 143). Give everyone a warm welcome and introduce the series saying something like this: *Welcome to 'Getting to Grips with God': a special course planned to help you get to grips with God and the basics of the Christian faith. Over the next ten weeks we will be dealing with such questions as* (shouted out by Question Mark):

- *Does God exist?*
- *Why am I alive?*
- *What's the big deal about Jesus?*
- *What's the point of being a Christian?*
- *What would it involve anyway?*

These headline questions should be shouted out by Question Mark, a newspaper-seller type dressed in coat, scarf and hat. Thank Mark for his questions and go on to set the scene for the meeting by explaining that today you will be *Getting to Grips with God* and dealing with such questions as (again shouted out by Question Mark):

- *What's God like?*
- *What's he do all day?*
- *Where is he?*
- *Who is he?*
- *How do we know he exists at all?*

Pick a quote

**Votes for
quotes**
3 mins

Explain to the group that you are going to read ten quotations about God and you want them to choose the one that is closest to their opinion about God. If possible get different leaders or young people, wearing different hats, to read each one. Run through the quotations a second time, so that everyone can check they've picked the right one. On the third run through ask the group members to raise a hand when their chosen quotation is read. Sum up by commenting on the distribution of votes.

The quotations

- *'God is dead'*
- *'I think God is just soooo groovy!'*
- *'If God exists he hasn't introduced himself to me yet.'*
- *'God is absolutely supercalafragalisticexpialidocious.'*
- *'God is just a cosy idea for oldies.'*
- *'God is.'*
- *'God is a rather boring subject.'*
- *'God is a seriously talented artist.'*
- *'God is whatever you want her to be.'*

Proving God's existence?

A telling tale
2 mins

It is of course impossible to prove that God exists but the evidence of the universe is pretty convincing. Dim the lights and tell or read the following story.

Once upon a time, a few hundred years ago, there lived a famous scientist who believed in God. Having spent his life studying the mysteries of life on earth he knew that it was God who was behind it all. There was simply no other convincing explanation. From floor to ceiling his dark and musty study was crammed with ancient leather-bound books, scientific equipment, microscopes and potted specimens. But upon his desk, in the middle of the room stood an exquisite model of our solar system. In the centre was the sun and revolving round it were the planets, Saturn, Venus, Mars, Earth, all operated by a wooden handle.

One day the famous scientist received a visit from a friend who did not share his belief in God. The friend noticed the beautiful model on the desk and, hoping to get one for himself, inquired who had made it. The scientist seized his opportunity and replied in all seriousness, 'I'm terribly sorry, did you say: Who made it?' 'Yes. Who made it? Where did you get it from?' the friend demanded. 'Well, nobody made it. I just came down here one morning and there it was sitting on my desk. Never seen it before in my life!' The friend was not amused, but the scientist continued to tease him: 'Honestly, I just found it on my desk, and it's been there ever since.' As the friend was getting extremely hot under the collar the twinkling-eyed scientist made his point. 'My dear friend,' he said, 'if you find it so hard to believe that this simple model can exist without someone who made it, how can you possibly believe that the real thing, which is infinitely more complex and wonderful, can exist without a God who made it?'

Facing the evidence

A mind-boggling multi-sensory experience
5 mins

In Romans 1 verse 20 St Paul tells us that *'Ever since God created the world, his invisible qualities, both his eternal power and his divine nature, have been clearly seen; they are perceived in the things that God has made.'* Like the scientist in the story, St Paul believed that our universe is convincing evidence for God's existence. The aim of this mind-boggling multi-sensory creation experience is to bring the group face to face with the wonder of the natural world in the hope that they too will conclude that God is the only explanation.

Get everyone sitting in a circle and if possible dim the lights. Explain to the group that the Bible tells us that the beautiful world in which we live is very good evidence for God's existence. Read Romans 1 verse 20 and explain that you are all about to undergo 'a mind-boggling, multi-sensory experience'. You will share various sensory experiences with the group and you want them to try and remember as much as possible about the textures, tastes, smells, sounds, feelings and images that they experience. Here is an outline of some things you could do to make up your mind-boggling, multi-sensory experience.

Darkness and light

Make the room as dark as possible and ask the group to think about how the darkness feels. Then light a candle in the middle of the room and encourage them to focus on the flame, on its brightness. How does it make them feel?

Water

In the candle-light go round the group with a bowl of water and a sponge and ask them to listen to the sound of the water. Let each person touch it or pour it over their hands. Ask them to think about how it feels. What is most striking about it?

Weather

In the semi-darkness play the weather sound effects on the audio cassette: rain, thunder, wind, summer garden (birds and insects), and sea lapping on the shore. There are 10 seconds of each. Ask them to close their eyes and let the sounds wash over them.

Go outside

Take the group outside, preferably into a garden. Get the group to look at the sky, the sun or stars and moon. Ask them to feel the wind, the warmth of the sun, or the sharp freshness of a cold night (depending on the time of day and year). Get them to touch the grass, the soil, the plants. Encourage them to smell the flowers and breathe the air, to look at the birds, insects and trees.

Taste

Back inside have some food chopped up: bits of apple, orange, carrot, etc. Pass it round and ask the group to ponder the taste, texture and smell of the food.

Animals

Show the group some photos or slides of animals, birds and fish if you can get hold of them. Try to emphasize the extraordinary diversity of the animal kingdom.

Each other

(For more mature groups!) Split the group into pairs and ask them to sit facing each other. Ask one of the pair to close their eyes then reach out their hands and touch their partner's face and hair, feeling the shapes and textures and then swap over. Then ask them to look into their partner's eyes and notice the amazing delicacy of the colour and patterns.

Summing up

Explain that the world in which we live is wonderfully beautiful and immensely complicated. Its very existence is strong evidence for the existence of God. Ask them to try and remember what the wind in the garden felt like. Make the point that even though they could not see the wind they could see the effect it had on the trees and they could feel it on their faces. In the same way, though we can't see God himself, we can see, in the beauty of the world, the things that he has done.

The Hot Seat

Interrogation time
4 mins

Set up the Hot Seat chair and the spot light and play the Hot Seat theme music on the audio cassette. Switch off the main lights and ask the selected leader to take his or her place in the Hot Seat. Explain to the group that each week they are going to have the opportunity to ask one of the leaders any questions they like about their personal experience of the subject of the meeting (in this case God). Set the ball rolling by asking a question or two yourself. Here are a couple you might like to try.

- *Why do you believe in God?*
- *Do you ever have any doubts about his existence?*

Then encourage everyone else to fire away too. Wind things up either when the questions run out or after about four minutes and give them a big clap. It doesn't matter if the inhabitant of the Hot Seat can't answer all the questions. It is important, however, that they are honest in their answers and talk about their personal experience.

Smash 'n' Grab

Getting the point
2 mins

Set up the back-lit Smash 'n' Grab screen and let Smash and Grab have the following conversation. Remember to exaggerate the hand gestures and watch carefully how the shadows look on the screen. That is all the group will see!

Grab: Hi, Smash! *(wave)*
Smash: Hi-ya, Grab! *(take five or shake hands)* 'Ow ya doin', mate?
Grab: Fine, thanks. *(thumbs up)*
Smash: 'Ave ya got the point, then?
Grab: The point of what? *(palm up)*
Smash: The point of the meetin'. *(pointing)*
Grab: Na, can't see it, mate. *(palm down)*
Smash: *(pointing)* Well, the point is that we know God exists because we can see the things he's made. We can see what he's like by lookin' at creation.
Grab: Oh right! Gotcha. This planet couldn't exist without God, so the world is evidence for God's existence. Now that you've pointed it out I can see it *(smash paper and grab point)*. I've got the point!
Smash: You've got it, mate. You've got the point! *(thumbs up)*

The questions box

An intro
1 min

Explain to the group that *Getting to Grips with God* is their chance to get the facts about the Christian faith straight for themselves. Encourage them to bring along all those nagging questions about the meaning of life that keep them awake at night and get them thrashed out at *Getting to Grips with God*. They shouldn't feel that any question is too simple to ask. Display the questions box (a shoe box with a hole in the top) and explain that all anonymous questions put in the box will be answered in the following meetings. If anyone wants to ask a more personal question they should write their name on the question slip and one of the leaders will chat through the answer with them on their own.

Activities

Getting to know each other

Fact files
5 mins

Hand each member of the group a copy of the worksheet and a pen (the masters for you to photocopy can be found on pages 123 and 124). Split them into pairs and ask them to complete the 'Getting to Know You' Fact File for their partner. This involves asking each other the following questions. Once they have had time to do this get back together and ask each person to introduce their partner by running through the facts in their file.

- Name
- Last thing eaten
- Pet details
- Favourite colour

- Most enjoyable experience
- Self-portrait in three words
- Ambitions

Hello, my name's GOD, I don't think you know me.

No, I'm not sure I do...

When I think of God . . .

First thoughts
2 mins

The aim of this activity is to help the group to identify their feelings and ideas about God so that they can see if their understanding of him has changed during the meeting. Give the group members about a minute to individually complete the 'When I think of God I think of...' section in the worksheet. Stress that the worksheets are private and no one else will see them.

Invent a God

This is a quick activity to help the group see the difference between gods invented by humans and God almighty (who invented humans). The point is that God is infinitely more wonderful, extraordinary and awesome than we could ever possibly imagine or invent.

Using the 'Invent a god' section of the worksheet, ask the group members to invent a god. It might help if you give them an example. Read out the details of the sun-god of ancient Egypt listed here.

Name:	Ra
Description:	Sun god of Ancient Egypt
Interesting facts:	Created himself from a mound in the primal ocean
	Born as a child every morning and dies at night as an old man
Appearance:	A falcon, with flame-spitting snake and sun disc round his head
Achievements:	Created mankind from his tears
Enemies:	Serpent Apep (always fighting)
3 words to sum up:	Frightening, judgment, death

Once everyone has invented their god, get them to unveil their creation to the rest of the group and discuss these together. Conclude (if appropriate) by making the point that they have created gods that are simply better or extreme versions of human beings. The reality is that God is inconceivably more wonderful, extraordinary and awesome than we could ever possibly imagine or invent.

Evidence please

Ask the group to think back to the mind-boggling, multi-sensory experience and jot down on the worksheet under the 'Natural Evidence' heading what they remember most clearly about the things they touched, tasted, smelt, heard and saw. They may like to discuss these. Then read Romans 1 verse 20 together on the sheet: *Ever since God created the world, his invisible qualities, both his eternal power and his divine nature, have been clearly seen; they are perceived in the things that God has made.*

As a way of exploring what the verse means put a selection of nature pictures taken from colour supplements or National Geographic magazines in a hat. (Photos of animals, landscapes, skies, sea, weather, deep space, flowers, insects, etc.) Ask each person to pick a photo and explain to the group what they think it tells us about what God is like.

- *A photo of a giraffe might tell us that God has a sense of humour.*
- *A photo of a desert might tell us that God has a wild streak to him.*
- *A photo of a waterfall might tell us that God is life-giving.*
- *A photo of deep space might tell us that God is immense.*
- *A photo of a ladybird or flower might tell us that God is very gentle.*
- *A photo of a parrot might tell us that God is colourful.*

What is God like?

This is a difficult word game exploring what the Bible tells us about God's character. Copy the sheet on the following page and cut it into cards. Ask a leader to pick a card and communicate to the rest of the group the characteristic of God written at the top of their card. They must do this without saying any of the words on the card. If they were trying to communicate that 'God is love', for example they must do this without saying the word 'love' or any word with 'love' in it such as 'loving'. Neither must they say the three words, 'heart', 'hate' or 'care'. Appoint a referee to check that the speaker doesn't use any of the banned words.

Once the rest of the group have guessed the characteristic of God, let someone else pick a card and have a go. If you want to make it more competitive see who can communicate the most God words in sixty seconds. Once you have had enough get the group members to write all the God words they can remember on their worksheets under the 'God is…' heading. This will provide them with a summary of what Christians believe about the nature of God.

Taking stock

Ask your group members to fill in the 'Taking stock' section of the worksheet. Then discuss what they have written together. The questions are as follows:

- *What has really struck you in this meeting?*
- *If you could ask God one question, what would you ask?*
- *Has your notion of God changed during this meeting? If so, how?*

Remind the group about the questions box and explain that they can either post anonymous questions to be answered to the whole group, or 'confidential' questions which will be answered privately. Suggest that they might choose to post the 'Taking stock' question they'd like to ask God.

Taking it further

Show or hand out copies of the *Getting to Grips with God* daily readings and encourage them to buy and use a copy during the week. Explain that the readings will help them get to grips with the issues that you are investigating in your *Getting to Grips with God* meetings. If you have enough copies perhaps you could select a reading and work through it together so that they get to grips with using them.

God is **Love**

- heart
- hate
- care

God is **Everywhere**

- all over
- wherever
- world

God is **Glorious**

- amazing
- shines
- wonderful

God is **True**

- false
- lie
- honest

God is **All-knowing**

- intelligent
- wise
- everything

God is **Forgiving**

- sorry
- sin
- forget

God is **Infinite**

- forever
- end
- limit

God is **Kind**

- help
- caring
- cruel

God is **Holy**

- perfect
- socks
- spirit

God is **Unchanging**

- same
- different
- always

God is **Faithful**

- promise
- trust
- reliable

God is **Patient**

- angry
- quick
- temper

God is **Fair**

- just
- judge
- right

God is **Lord**

- king
- master
- ruler

God is **King**

- queen
- ruler
- throne

God is **Merciful**

- pardon
- forgive
- punish

God is **Creator**

- world
- nature
- make

God is **Eternal**

- forever
- never-ending
- infinite

God is **All-powerful**

- anything
- do
- electricity

God is **Good**

- kind
- bad
- right

God is **Pure**

- perfect
- clean
- good

God is **Perfect**

- wrong
- faultless
- 100 %

God is **Judge**

- jury
- court
- crime

God is **Loyal**

- faithful
- friend
- reliable

Getting to Grips
with Life

2

The Aim: To see that we were created by God to be his friends, but have turned away from him.

The Lightning Bolt: Genesis 1:26–31 and Romans 3:23.
The creation of the human race 'in God's image' & our subsequent fall into sin.

Equipment Checklist:

PRESENTATIONS
- ❏ theme music
- ❏ Question Mark outfit
- ❏ broadcast backing tracks
- ❏ red & green card for each person
- ❏ funky chicken backing track
- ❏ Hot Seat, light & theme tune
- ❏ Smash 'n' Grab kit
- ❏ questions box

ACTIVITIES
- ❏ worksheets & pens
- ❏ God word slips in hat
- ❏ video
- ❏ copies of daily readings

Letter to leaders

The Bible tells us that God created human beings 'in his image'. This doesn't mean that we *look* like him, but rather that we share in his characteristics. As evidence for this, C.S. Lewis points to the extraordinary moral consensus throughout world history. He lists texts from ancient Norse, Egyptian, Roman, Hebrew and Indian manuscripts all agreeing that it is wrong to murder, to commit adultery, to lie, slander or be cowardly, and that it is right to be loyal and look after your children and the poor. The only explanation for this agreement, says C.S. Lewis, is that it comes from an 'in-built' moral sense that is an expression of God's character in us.[2]

Despite our divine origins we humans have gone spectacularly off the rails. A quick flick through the newspaper reveals that God's image in each of us has been distorted and ruined. We may know right from wrong, but we seem to prefer the latter. We have all turned from God and are on the road to ruin. The parallel of the ruined building is actually very helpful. We are like once magnificent buildings, now uninhabited and falling into a state of decay. Within the ruins you can still catch a glimpse of the building's former glory, the traces of God's image. The good news is that God is the master renovator and, when we invite him, he moves back into his ruined home and begins the work of restoration.

- **Remember that even though renovation can be painful, it's very worthwhile.**

Presentations

 ## Headline questions

**Welcome &
introduction
2 mins**

Create a warm, friendly atmosphere and have the *Getting to Grips with God* theme music playing as the group arrives (on audio tape—see page 143). Welcome everyone and introduce the series saying something like this: *Welcome to 'Getting to Grips with God', a special course planned to help you get to grips with God and the basics of the Christian faith. Over the next nine weeks we will be dealing with such questions as* (shouted out by Question Mark):

- *Does God exist?*
- *Why am I alive?*
- *What's the big deal about Jesus?*
- *What's the point of being a Christian?*
- *What would it involve anyway?*

Thank Mark for his questions and go on to set the scene for the second *Getting to Grips with God* meeting. Explain that today you will be Getting to Grips with Life and dealing with such questions as (again shouted out by Question Mark):

- *Why am I alive?*
- *What's the meaning of life?*
- *What makes a human human?*
- *What's God got to do with it?*
- *Why is the world in such a mess?*

 ## Celebrating the human race . . .

**A promotion
2 mins**

Run this brief broadcast on behalf of the human race. It celebrates some of the great achievements of human beings and portrays the race in a very rosy light. Play the backing track on the audio cassette (see page 143) and read the script in a deep, slow voice.

The most remarkable inhabitant of planet earth is the human being. Over the last million years the human race has made quite astonishing leaps of progress, attaining ever higher pinnacles of achievement. They dominate the planet through their immense intellectual powers and ability to communicate in over 4,000 different languages. They have developed structures of society through which they provide for all their needs: food, housing, transport, education, health care, and social justice. They have enriched their lives with exquisite masterpieces of art, music, poetry and literature. In the realm of science and technology humans have pushed back frontier after frontier, even to the point of travelling in deep space and setting foot on the moon. The poet Bill Shakespeare summed up the miracle of the human race when he said, 'What a piece of work is a man! How noble in reason! How infinite in faculty! In form, in moving, how express and admirable! In action how like an angel! In apprehension how like a god! The beauty of the world! The paragon of animals!'[3]

Beware—human beings

A human warning
2 mins

Follow the positive broadcast on the human race with this short warning about the dangers posed by human beings. Play the backing track on the cassette and read the script in a fast, serious and warning voice.

Danger—this is a warning about human beings. Though appearing harmless, human beings can be extremely dangerous—yes, DANGEROUS. These wicked, scheming two-legged beings are capable of horrific atrocities—yes, HORRIFIC ATROCITIES. We have worldwide records of rape, murder, ethnic cleansing, torture, child abuse, extreme violence, cruelty to animals, destruction of the environment, selfishness, greed, exploitation, corruption, racism and war. If you think you see a human being, do not approach it but call the Planet Protection Police immediately on 01 101010. The threat posed by the human animal is too dangerous to ignore. Take action now to protect your life and your planet.

Human beings

Right & wrong?
4 mins

Explain to the group that, having seen the best and the worst about human beings, you are going to investigate the rights and wrongs of human behaviour a little further. Give each person two small cards, one red and the other green. Explain that you are going to read ten examples of human behaviour and you want them to indicate whether the behaviour is good or bad. They do this by showing the red card for bad behaviour and the green for good. Read each situation, pause and then count to three. On the count of three each person is to hold up their chosen card.

The situations

1. On discovering a wallet containing £20 Alf Adams took it to the local police station.

2. Billy Brown accidentally dropped and broke his new personal stereo. As there was no sign of the accident he took it back to the shop, claiming that it had never worked and asked for it to be replaced or repaired under guarantee.

3. A good friend of Diane Dixon has become very famous. Diane received a call from a journalist offering loads of money for juicy information about her friend's past, but she refused to take the dosh and spill the beans.

4. Fyona Fare was walking home on a cold winter's day when she saw an old lady slip over on the pavement. She was in a bit of a hurry to get home for her favourite TV programme so she pretended she hadn't seen the accident.

5. Gary Gap was with his mates when they started making racist remarks about a boy in the class. Gary went along with it because he didn't want to lose his mates.

6. Mr and Mrs Henry Hall had been invited to the party of a life-time. Unfortunately, they couldn't find a babysitter so they left their two children aged 6 and 8 alone at home once they'd gone off to sleep.

7. Jerry Jones heard on the grapevine that his form tutor was going out with the head's daughter. He thought that this was much too juicy to keep to himself so he passed the word on to the rest of the form.

8. When Kerry King saw her best friend being beaten up by the school bullies she waded in there to try and rescue her.

9. Larry Lane had a foul day. When he got home his Mum annoyed him by asking how his day was so he called her an interfering old bag.

10. On his way to spend a fiver on the lottery Eustace Edwards passed a person collecting money for famine relief in Africa. He resisted the temptation to help the starving and bought his tickets anyway.

If the group vote seriously they should be virtually unanimous about which behaviour was right and which was wrong. Point this out to them and ask why they think this is. Why do we all agree about what is right and what is wrong? Make the point that there is worldwide agreement about what is right and wrong. All round the world, all through the centuries people have agreed that it's wrong to murder, but it's good to help the poor. It's wrong to go off with someone else's wife, but it's good to look after your family. It's wrong to be a coward, but it's good to tell the truth. It's wrong to spread false rumours, but it's good to look after your parents in their old age. The reason for this amazing agreement is that we human beings are made in God's image to be like him. Read Genesis 1 verses 26–31 to the group and explain that we agree about right and wrong because we were made sharing God's character and so have his sense of right and wrong built into us.

Fred the Funky Chicken

A quest for the meaning of life

3 mins

Take the group on a quest for the meaning of life with Fred the Funky Chicken. Either read this poem or perform it as a rap using the backing track on the audio cassette. If you feel like dressing up as a chicken (pink rubber glove on head) and strutting round flapping your arms, so much the better. The text printed in **bold** is dialogue to be thrown in by someone listening to the story. Change the names marked with an * as appropriate.

I once had a friend, a funky chicken called Fred
And I remember an interesting thing he once said.
He said, 'Jo*, I've been thinking—I really want more
Than just to strut round and peck corn off the floor!'

Fred the Funky Chicken had his eye on us lot
And wanted to find out what it was we had got.
'I'm going on a quest,' he said, 'I have to be quite sure
What gives human beings that crucial something more.'

He started off with gambling and played with real flair
Until Fred the Gambling Chicken became Fred the Millionaire.
He brought himself a mansion, a sports car and yacht
But still he had a feeling there was more he hadn't got.

What! You mean that being rich didn't make him happy? Why ever not?
Because there is more to life than money, as Fred was soon to find out…

His plan was to see the world, he'd travel far and wide,
From England to Australia and back round the other side.
He returned from his journey with souvenirs galore,
Plus a nasty stomach bug, but not that something more.

Next he thought, 'I'll be famous with my own show on TV,
Chatting to world superstars for everyone to see!'
But even talking to Madonna* he found a real bore
It wasn't what he wanted and not that something more.

Hang on a tick, Jo*! Are you saying that, even though Fred was a world-famous celeb, he still felt there was something missing from his life?
Yep, that's right. There's more to life than fame and fortune.

Then Fred thought, 'I know what's missing in my life:
What I have to do now is find myself a wife.'
So when Fred met Wilamina they were married that same day
But he hadn't found life's meaning (much to his dismay).

So when I last saw Fred he was almost in despair,
So I said, 'Fred, I've found life's meaning, let me tell you where;
Not in fame, or fortune, travel or a wife.
There's something more important that you can do in life.'

What! You're saying that fame and fortune didn't make him happy and neither did travel or true love! Well, frankly I'm amazed. So what was it, Jo*?

'The meaning of all human life is to be God's friend;
It really is the only way to be happy in the end.'
'At last,' crowed Fred, 'I see it! So it's God I'm looking for!
You could've saved me hassle if you'd told me that before!'

So Fred's quest for life's meaning was at last now done.
He went back to his henhouse knowing God's the only one
Who gives life its real meaning, he's that 'something more',
And he settled down to strut round with more purpose than before.

The Hot Seat

Interrogation time
4 mins

Set up the Hot Seat and the lamp and play the Hot Seat music on the audio cassette. Explain to the group that this is their opportunity to grill the inhabitant of this week's Hot Seat about their understanding of the meaning of life. If necessary set the ball rolling with a question or two of your own:

- *Why do you think God made you like you are?*
- *What do you think is the meaning of life and why?*

Smash 'n' Grab

Getting the point
1 min

Set up the back-lit Smash 'n' Grab screen and let Smash and Grab have the following conversation. Remember to exaggerate the gestures and watch carefully how the shadows look on the screen. That is all the group will see!

Grab: Hi, Smash! *(wave)*
Smash: Hi-ya, Grab! *(shake hands)* 'Ow ya doin', mate?
Grab: Fine thanks. *(thumbs up)*
Smash: 'Ave ya got the point, then?
Grab: The point of what? *(palm up)*
Smash: The point of the meetin'.
Grab: Na, can't see it, mate. *(palm down)*
Smash: *(pointing)* Well, the point is that we 'uman beings were made by God to be like 'im and be 'is mates. That's why we're alive.
Grab: Oh right! Gotcha. So the answer to the question, 'Why am I alive?' is 'To be friends with the God who made me.' Now that you've pointed it out, I can see it. *(Smash paper and grab point.)* I've got the point!
Smash: You've got it, mate. You've got the point! *(thumbs up)*

Any answers

Qs & As
2 mins

Answer any questions that were put in the box at the last meeting. At the end of this book there are outline answers to ten commonly asked questions. Remind everyone about the box and encourage them to post their queries.

Activities

If I were a . . .

What are you like?
5 mins

Give everyone the chance to chat for a few minutes and then play the following icebreaker game to help them think about what makes them who they are. Ask each group member to imagine themselves as a tree. What kind of tree would they be? Knarled old oak, baby Christmas tree, weeping willow, beach tree, or glistening silver birch. Share these thoughts with each other and then ask them what kind of animal they would be: porcupine, piranha, parrot, Pekinese or penguin? Finally, ponder together which month of the year you would all be. This will give you some interesting insights into both yourself and your group members.

Why are we alive?

Telling stories
10 mins

Hand everyone a copy of the worksheets (master copies are on pages 125 and 126) and read Genesis 1:26–31 together. You might need to explain that Genesis is not a scientific text-book account of the creation of humans. It deals more with the 'why' than the 'how' of human existence. Ask them to try and sum up what this poetic account of the creation of humans tells us about why we are alive under the 'Why are we alive?' heading.

Go on to explore what it means to be created to be like God. Write out the ten God words listed below on separate slips of paper and put them in a hat. Split the group into pairs and ask each to pick out one of the God words. Explain that you want them to improvise a little scene in which a person shows that God quality in their life. E.g. if the God word was 'fair', they might act out an example of someone sharing their sweets fairly. Run through each sketch and ask the others to guess which God characteristic they were showing. Sum up by explaining that being made to be like God means that we were made to be loving, kind, loyal, just, etc. like God.

- fair
- good
- kind
- loyal
- forgiving
- patient
- loving
- merciful
- faithful
- creative

An alternative would be to get each person to pick a God word and then go round the group improvising a story about a day in the life of Jo Bloggs. Explain that you will each have fifteen seconds to contribute an incident in the day in the life of Jo Bloggs in which he or she demonstrates the God quality on their piece of paper. When you ring a bell every fifteen seconds the next person in the circle has to carry on exactly where the last person left off.

Would you do what you should?

A quiz
5 mins

The following activity aims to make the point that though we all have this Godly in-built sense of right and wrong we fail to live up to it. Ask everyone to turn to their worksheets and complete the 'What would you do?' questionnaire. This involves ticking 'yes' or 'no' boxes to indicate what they *would* do in ten situations parallel to those described in the presentation section. They then have to indicate what they *should* have done in each situation. Ask them to work out in how many of the situations would they have done what they should. In other words in how many questions did they tick two 'Yes' or two 'No' boxes. Conclude by pointing out that though we know what we should do we don't always do it. The questions are as follows:

1. *You find a wallet containing £20. Would you keep the dosh?*
2. *You drop your new personal stereo and break it. As there is no visible damage would you try and claim the repairs under the guarantee?*
3. *A good friend has become very famous. A journalist offers you loads of money for juicy information about their past. Would you take it and tell all?*
4. *On a cold winter's day you see an old lady slip over on the pavement. Would you try to help?*

5. One of your friends makes a racist remark. Would you say anything?

6. You have been invited to the party of a life-time. You can't find a babysitter for your six- and eight-year-old kids. Do you leave them by themselves?

7. You hear that your form tutor has started going out with the head's daughter/son. Would you pass it round the class?

8. At school you see your best mate being beaten up. Would you try to help?

9. You've had a bad day. When you get home your Mum says something harmless that you find very annoying. Would you get ratty?

10. You were on your way to spend a fiver on the lottery when you see a person collecting money for famine relief. Would you give the £5 to feed the hungry?

What's gone wrong?

Life on video
4 min

To help the group appreciate the extent to which we all fail to live up to our own standards (let alone God's) ask them to imagine that you have got their whole life recorded on video. Hold up a blank video to add to the effect. Ask them to think about which bits would they be happy to have screened on prime-time TV and which bits would they pay a lot of dosh not to be seen. It would be a bit much to ask them to give you details, but suggest they fill in the pie chart in the worksheet with the percentages of 'definitely not' hours, 'don't mind' hours and 'quite pleased' hours. Conclude by making the point that despite our best efforts not much of our lives are up to scratch. Perhaps you could then read Romans 3 verse 23 together from the worksheet.

Parents and children

Great expectations
4 mins

Ask the group members to try and imagine that they and their partner are just about to start a family. They have decorated the baby's room, put up the mobiles and bought in six tonnes of nappies. Go on to discuss the following questions:

● What would you most look forward to about being a parent?
● What kind of start in life would you hope to give to your child?
● How would you expect your child to treat you as they grew up?
● What qualities you would hope for in a good son or daughter?
● How would you feel if your kid turned into a right little thug who didn't care about you at all?

Conclude by explaining that God is like a parent and we are his children. Ask the group to consider if the feelings he must have about us rebellious kids are any different to how they'd feel if their children didn't care at all about them.

In God's shoes

Answers on a postcard
4 mins

Ask the group to put themselves in God's shoes and decide what he should do about the fact that we human beings, though knowing the difference between right and wrong, so often choose wrong? What should he do about the fact that his children so often don't care about him at all? What should he do about the mess the human race is in? Ask them to write their suggestions on the postcard on the worksheet. Perhaps you could go on to discuss these together. Conclude by explaining that you will be investigating what God actually did in the next two *Getting to Grips with God* meetings.

Taking stock

The crunch
2 mins

Finish by asking the group to answer the questions listed under the 'Taking stock' heading on the worksheet. If there is time perhaps you could discuss these together. The questions are as follows:

● *What have you discovered about the meaning of life?*
● *What's gone wrong with the human race?*

Feedback on the readings

Ask your group how they are getting on with the *Getting to Grips with God* daily readings. Do encourage them to keep going, or to give them a go if they haven't tried them yet. Also remind them to post any questions they have into the questions box.

Getting to Grips
with Jesus

The Aim: To discover that Jesus was God living a human life.

The Lightning Bolt: John 11:17–45.
Jesus raises Lazarus.

Equipment Checklist

PRESENTATIONS
- ❏ theme music
- ❏ Question Mark outfit
- ❏ large sheet of paper & pens
- ❏ backing music for ten true facts
- ❏ game show cards
- ❏ Hot Seat, light & theme tune
- ❏ Smash 'n' Grab kit
- ❏ questions box

ACTIVITIES
- ❏ worksheets & pens
- ❏ coin & plasticine
- ❏ large sheets of paper
- ❏ copies of daily readings

Letter to leaders

Imagine this: whilst travelling home on the bus one day you get chatting to a man sitting next to you. You end up having a frank and open conversation. He gives you a lot to think about and you find his company quite different from any you have enjoyed before. Just before you get off you realize that you don't know his name. He tells you that his name is Alpha Centurae Draco Minor, a being from a distant galaxy, visiting planet earth in human form. He is obviously not joking and you are surprisingly convinced. How would your family respond when you told them about your encounter on the bus?

This may sound far-fetched, but it is not that different from what Christians believe about Jesus Christ. In truth Christian belief is far more extraordinary; we believe that Jesus is none other than God Almighty, creator of the universe, visiting planet earth in a human body. I continually find myself taking this awesome truth for granted, putting it in the same 'interesting facts' category as dinosaurs or gravity. It is said that 'familiarity breeds contempt' and I fear that is sometimes true of my response to Jesus. May God use this meeting to open our eyes once again to the awesome identity of Jesus.

● *Spend some time thinking about the fact that Jesus is God in a human body. Ask God to re-open your eyes to the extraordinary implications of this fact and then talk to him about it.*

Presentations

Headline questions

**Welcome &
introduction**
1 min

Have the *Getting to Grips with God* theme music playing as the group arrives and, as they do so, get everyone to jot down their date of birth on a large sheet of paper. Once everyone has settled and you have collected all the dates, give the group a warm welcome and ask them what the dates all have in common. The answer is that they are all dated from the birth of a man called Jesus. The whole calendar of the Western world is centred round a man who lived nearly 2,000 years ago. That man stands right at the heart of the Christian faith. Conclude by saying that in today's meeting you will be getting to grips with Jesus and grappling with such questions as (again shouted out by Question Mark):

- *What's the big deal about Jesus?*
- *What did he do?*
- *Was he mad, bad or God?*
- *Why are we still talking about him today?*
- *What's he got to do with me?*

Ten true facts about Jesus

Fact parade
2 mins

This presentation aims to give the group a lively introduction to ten undisputed facts about Jesus. Play the 'ten true facts' backing track on the audio cassette and read each of the ten facts between each of the stabs. Perhaps two leaders could read alternate facts, or one could call out the numbers and the other give the facts.

1. *We know more about the life of Jesus than any other figure in the ancient world.*
2. *He was a Jew who lived in Palestine about 2,000 years ago.*
3. *He never married but worked as a carpenter and builder until he was about thirty.*
4. *At thirty he left home and became a travelling preacher, healer and miracle worker.*
5. *He mixed with the outcasts of society and had a band of disciples who followed him.*
6. *He claimed to be the Son of God.*
7. *He was arrested and tried on charges of blasphemy and executed by crucifixion.*
8. *Two days later his tomb was found to be empty.*
9. *The Bible records eleven separate encounters with Jesus after his death and more than 500 witnesses.*
10. *Ever since, millions of people have believed that he is alive today.*

The big news

**A telling
incident**
6 mins

This is a look at a telling incident in Jesus' life that reveals five key truths about him:

- *He is the giver of life*
- *He is the Son of God*
- *He cares about people*
- *He has a hot-line to God*
- *He can raise the dead*

Ask for between two and six volunteers, split them into two teams and sit them behind two tables at the front. Give each team five cards on which are written the five key truths above. Also give each team some kind of buzzer, bell or whistle. Explain that you are going to read the account of an incident in Jesus' life that reveals these five things about Jesus. As soon as the team members spot the part of the story that makes any of the five points they are to blow their whistle and hold up the appropriate card. If they are correct they get a point, but if they are wrong they lose one.

Read to the group the account of Jesus raising Lazarus in John 11:17–44. To add effect read it in the following parts: NARRATOR, MARTHA, JESUS, MARY, OTHERS. As soon as either team buzzes, stop the story and award or subtract points as appropriate. Then start again exactly where you left off. Conclude by reading through the five points and emphasizing that the story reveals that Jesus was none other than God living a human life.

One solitary life

The life of Jesus
2 mins

Ask the group to sit quietly with their eyes closed and read them this short passage about the life of Jesus and its massive consequences.

He was born of Jewish parents in an obscure village—the child of a peasant woman. He grew up in another obscure village where he worked in a carpenter's shop until he was thirty, and then for three years became a travelling preacher.

He never wrote a book; he never held office; he never owned a house; he never had a family. He never went to college; he never put his foot inside a big city. He never travelled two hundred miles from the place where he was born. He never did one of the things that usually accompany greatness. He had no credentials but himself.

While he was a young man, the tide of popular opinion turned against him. His friends ran away; one betrayed him; one denied him. He was turned over to his enemies and went through a mockery of a trial.

He was nailed to a cross between two thieves. His executioners gambled for the only piece of property he owned on earth—and that was his robe.

When he was dead he was taken down and laid in a borrowed grave, through the pity of a friend.

Nineteen centuries have come and gone and today he is the centre-piece of the human race and the leader of the column of progress.

I am well within the mark when I say that all the armies that ever marched, all the navies that ever sailed the seas, all the parliaments that ever sat and all the kings that ever reigned put together have not affected the life of man on earth as powerfully as has that one solitary life.

Anonymous

The Hot Seat

Interrogation time
4 mins

Set up the Hot Seat, switch on the spotlight and play the Hot Seat backing music. Then introduce the occupier of today's Hot Seat. Explain that this is the group's one and only opportunity to grill the selected leader about his or her personal experience of Jesus, and the difference he has made to his or her life. It really doesn't matter if the questions cover a broader range of topics than this. It is good for the group to have the opportunity to find out about someone else's journey with God. Here are some questions you might like to use to set the ball rolling:

- *How did you come to believe that Jesus is the Son of God?*
- *How would your life be different if you didn't know about Jesus?*
- *What particularly appeals to you about him?*

Smash 'n' Grab

Getting the
point
1 min

Set up the back-lit Smash 'n' Grab screen and hold the following conversation or something like it. Remember to exaggerate the gestures and watch carefully how the shadows look on the screen. That is all the group will see!

Grab: Hi, Smash! *(wave)*

Smash: Hi-ya, Grab! *(shake hands)* 'Ow ya doin', mate?

Grab: Not too bad, not too bad. *(thumbs up)*

Smash: 'Ave ya got the point, then?

Grab: The point of what? *(palm up)*

Smash: The point of the meetin'.

Grab: Na, can't see it, mate. *(palm down)*

Smash: *(pointing)* Well, the point is that 2,000 years ago God invaded planet earth in the person of Jesus.

Grab: Oh right! So Jesus was God living a human life and when we look at Jesus we see what God is like. I can see it now that you've pointed it out. *(Smash paper and grab point.)* I've got the point!

Smash: You've got it, mate. You've got the point! *(thumbs up)*

Any answers

Qs & As
2 mins

If there are any questions in the questions box from last week, answer one or two of them as simply and clearly as you can. Do encourage the group to post any other questions they have. See page 115 for sample answers to common questions.

Activities

Match 'n' mix

Pairing up
5 mins

Ask everyone to think of their favourite person or personal hero. Then get everyone to pair up with someone else who has a different hero or favourite. Ask them to work out what kind of person you would get if you blended, crossed or mixed these two characters together. Hand out copies of the worksheets and ask them to fill in the Match 'n' Mix section. See below for what you might get if you match 'n' mix Prince Charles and Eric Cantona. Once everyone has had time to match 'n' mix their heroes ask the group to share their creations.

Match 'n' Mix:	*Prince Charles & Eric Cantona*
Name:	*Prince Cantona*
Age:	*35-ish*
Character:	*fiery temper with a touch of class*
Favourite expression:	*'Off with his head!'*
Hobbies:	*painting, kung fu*
Profession:	*celebrity*
Fashion style:	*sunglasses, stubble and crown*
Favourite pop group:	*Royal Mexican Wave*
Ultimate ambition:	*Supreme ruler of the kingdom of soccer*

The God–man

**Match 'n' mix
God 'n' man**
5 mins

Ask the group what you would get if you matched 'n' mixed God and a human being. Turn to the worksheets again and get them to fill in the table with their thoughts about what a God–man would be like. It might help if you look at the list of 'God words' from the first meeting. These are listed below. You may prefer to do this as a group and discuss together what your comments under each heading should be. If so, draw out an enlarged version of the table on a large sheet of paper and get someone to fill it in as you go along.

- *love*
- *true*
- *infinite*
- *unchanging*
- *fair*
- *merciful*
- *all-powerful*
- *perfect*

- *everywhere*
- *all-knowing*
- *kind*
- *faithful*
- *Lord*
- *creator*
- *good*
- *judge*

- *glorious*
- *forgiving*
- *holy*
- *patient*
- *king*
- *eternal*
- *pure*
- *loyal*

The Jesus fact race

A quiz
8 mins

Explain to the group that Christians believe that Jesus was this God–man; that he was God living a human life. Take a coin and press it into some plasticene making an imprint. Explain that Jesus is the imprint of God on human flesh (Hebrews 1:3). Say that you are now going to find out how much the group knows about Jesus the God–man. Split them into teams of about four and give them each four pens and a large sheet of paper divided into four boxes. Label each box with one of the following titles:

- *Personal details (from birth to death)*
- *Parables*
- *Miracles*
- *Claims of Jesus*

Explain that each team has four minutes to try and list as much as possible under each of the four headings. They are to list as many of Jesus' miracles, parables, claims and personal details as they can. You might like to suggest that they all work on different boxes and change round every minute. When time is up bring the groups back together and run through the lists and see who has the longest list of valid examples.

A telling incident

**The raising of
Lazarus**
10 mins

Explain to the group that you are going to take a look at a very telling incident from the life of Jesus. It is found in John 11:17–44 and is written out below and on the worksheets. Explain to the group that Mary and Martha were friends of Jesus, and their brother Lazarus had recently died. The story begins when Jesus comes to see them. Read it together with different group members reading the parts of NARRATOR, MARTHA, JESUS, PERSON 1 & PERSON 2.

Narrator:	When Jesus arrived, he found that Lazarus had been buried four days before. When Martha heard that Jesus was coming, she went out to meet him.
Martha:	If you had been here, Lord, my brother would not have died! But I know that even now God will give you whatever you ask him for.
Jesus:	Your brother will rise to life.
Martha:	I know that he will rise to life on the last day.
Jesus:	I am the resurrection and the life. Those who believe in me will live, even though they die; and all those who live and believe in me will never die. Do you believe this?
Martha:	Yes, Lord! I do believe that you are the Messiah, the Son of God, who was to come into the world.
Narrator:	When Jesus saw her weeping, and saw how the people who were with her were weeping also, his heart was touched, and he was deeply moved.
Jesus:	Where have you buried him?
Person 1:	Come and see, Lord.
Narrator:	Jesus wept.
Person 1:	See how much he loved him!
Person 2:	He gave sight to the blind man, didn't he? Could he not have kept Lazarus from dying?
Narrator:	Deeply moved once more, Jesus went to the tomb, which was a cave with a stone placed at the entrance.
Jesus:	Take the stone away!
Martha:	There will be a bad smell, Lord. He has been buried four days!
Jesus:	Didn't I tell you that you would see God's glory if you believed?
Narrator:	They took the stone away. Jesus looked up to heaven.
Jesus:	I thank you, Father, that you listen to me. I know that you always listen to me, but I say this for the sake of the people here, so that they will believe that you sent me. (Pause and then in a loud voice) Lazarus, come out!
Narrator:	He came out, his hands and feet wrapped in grave clothes, and with a cloth round his face.
Jesus:	Untie him and let him go.
Narrator:	Many of the people who had come to visit Mary and Martha saw what Jesus did, and they believed in him.

Ask the group what strikes them about Jesus from this event? Suggest that they read through it again and highlight any key sentences. Share your thoughts together and suggest that they note down these discoveries about Jesus in the 'Discoveries' section of their worksheets. The important facts about Jesus that this event reveals include:

- Jesus is 'the giver of life'
- Jesus is 'the Son of God who has come into the world'
- He is gentle and compassionate
- He has a hot-line to God
- He can bring the dead back to life

Go on to hold a newspaper headline competition. Explain that you want them to think up punchy newspaper headlines for each of the five points. Then go round the group shouting them out rather as Question Mark does at the beginning of each meeting. For example,

'PREACHER WEEPS IN PUBLIC' or 'GOD COMES TO TOWN'. As a group choose the best headline for each point.

Taking stock

Mad, bad or God?
5 mins

Ask the group members to turn to their worksheets again and fill in the 'Taking stock' section. Remind them that, in his conversation with Martha, Jesus accepted her statement that he was the Son of God who has come into the world. At other times Jesus made that shocking statement about himself and there are only three ways of explaining it. Either he was a liar in claiming to be God, or he was mad and was totally deceived himself, or he was telling the truth and *was* the Son of God who had come into the world. Ask the group to tick the box that they think best explains Jesus' extraordinary claim and then answer the other two questions. Perhaps you could discuss these together.

● *Why do you think people are still following Jesus 2,000 years on?*
● *Has anything particularly struck you in this meeting? What is it and why?*

Any questions

A reminder
I min

Remind the group about the questions box and encourage them to write down and post their questions. Perhaps you could ask them how they are getting on with their daily readings and encourage them to keep going.

Getting to Grips with
the Rescue

4

The Aim: To understand that Jesus died to take the punishment from God that we deserve, and that God raised him again.

The Lightning Bolt: Matthew 27:11–54 & John 20:1–18.
The crucifixion and the resurrection.

Equipment Checklist

PRESENTATIONS
- ❏ theme music
- ❏ Question Mark outfit
- ❏ crucifixion reading backing track
- ❏ gun, bus, chick
- ❏ Hot Seat, light & theme music
- ❏ Smash 'n' Grab kit
- ❏ resurrection backing track
- ❏ phone & phone sound effects
- ❏ questions box

ACTIVITIES
- ❏ worksheet & pens
- ❏ sticky labels
- ❏ crucifixion backing track
- ❏ wooden spoon

Letter to leaders

I'm sure that most people would agree that justice should be done. It is right that those who commit crimes should be punished and the innocent should be protected. If a crime had been committed against a member of your family (perhaps someone had been pushing drugs on your child) you would have a right to expect that this person be punished. Certainly they should not be let off with a pat on the head and a 'There, there, we all make mistakes!'

It's comforting to know that God is a God of justice. Imagine the public outrage if the press reliably discovered that a judge had said to some war criminals on trial, 'There, there, never mind, we all make mistakes!' The reality is that God's standards of right and wrong are far more exacting than ours. God expects perfection from every human being and we have all failed to live up to his requirements. His divine justice awaits us all. Fair's fair.

I don't think I will ever fully understand how Jesus' death meets the demands of God's justice. It's sometimes described as our debt being paid, our punishment being taken by one who had no guilt. Understanding it fully, however, is not vital—it's accepting it that counts. And millions of Christians over the centuries have found that the events of that terrible Friday have freed them from guilt and given them the confidence to believe that God has forgiven and accepted them as his blameless children.

- **When was the last time you thanked Jesus for his astonishing sacrifice for you?**

Presentations

This meeting is structured slightly differently to the others. Start off with presentations to the group about the death of Jesus and then split into activity groups to explore it further. Then join back together for the final 15 minutes and present the fantastic fact of the resurrection.

Leading questions

Welcome & introduction
1 min

Play the *Getting to Grips with God* theme music as the group arrives. Give them a warm welcome and remind them how in the last meeting you discovered that Jesus was none other than God living a human life. Go on to say that today you'll be thinking about his death and resurrection and grappling with such questions as (shouted out by Question Mark):

- *Why was Jesus nailed?*
- *What's it got to do with me?*
- *Who nicked the body?*
- *Did Jesus rise again?*
- *If so, where's the evidence?*

The death of Jesus

A reading
3 mins

Ask everyone to get themselves comfortable, then dim the lights and read to the group Matthew's account of the death of Jesus (Matthew 27:11–54). This is very effective if it is read by two people as outlined below (preferably a man reading the bold text and a woman reading the italic). Play the backing track on the audio cassette as you read.

Jesus stood before the Roman Governor, who questioned him. 'Are you the king of the Jews?' he asked.

'So you say,' answered Jesus.

But he said nothing in response to the accusations of the chief priests and elders. So Pilate said to him,

'Don't you hear all these things they accuse you of?'

But Jesus refused to answer a single word, with the result that the Governor was greatly surprised.

At every Passover Festival the Roman Governor was in the habit of setting free any one prisoner the crowd asked for. At that time there was a well-known prisoner named Jesus Barabbas. So when the crowd gathered, Pilate asked them, 'Which one do you want me to set free for you? Jesus Barabbas or Jesus called the Messiah?' He knew very well that the Jewish authorities had handed Jesus over to him because they were jealous.

While Pilate was sitting in the judgement hall, his wife sent him a message: 'Have nothing to do with that innocent man, because in a dream last night I suffered much on account of him.' The chief priests and the elders persuaded the crowd to ask Pilate to set Barabbas free and have Jesus put to death.

But Pilate asked the crowd, 'Which one of these two do you want me to set free for you?'

'BARABBAS!' they answered.

'What, then, shall I do with Jesus called the Messiah?'

'CRUCIFY HIM!'

'What crime has he committed?'

Then they started shouting at the top of their voices: 'CRUCIFY HIM!'

When Pilate saw that it was no use to go on, but that a riot might break out, he took some water, washed his hands in front of the crowd, and said, 'I am not responsible for the death of this man! This is your doing!'

The whole crowd answered, 'Let the responsibility for his death fall on us and our children!'

Then Pilate set Barabbas free for them; and after he had Jesus whipped, he handed him over to be crucified.

Then Pilate's soldiers took Jesus into the governor's palace, and the whole company gathered round him.

They stripped off his clothes and put a scarlet robe on him.

Then they made a crown out of thorny branches and placed it on his head,

and put a stick in his right hand; then they knelt before him and mocked him.

(read together) 'LONG LIVE THE KING OF THE JEWS!' they said.

They spat on him, and took the stick and hit him over the head.

When they had finished mocking him, they took the robe off and put his own clothes back on him. Then they led him out to crucify him.

As they were going out, they met a man from Cyrene named Simon, and the soldiers forced him to carry Jesus' cross. They came to a place called Golgotha, which means, 'The Place of the Skull'. There they offered Jesus wine mixed with a bitter substance; but after tasting it, he would not drink it. They crucified him and then divided his clothes among them by throwing dice. After that they sat there and watched him. Above his head they put the written notice of the accusation against him: 'This is Jesus, the King of the Jews.'

Then they crucified two bandits with Jesus, one on his right and the other on his left. People passing by shook their heads and hurled insults at Jesus:

'You were going to tear down the Temple and build it up again in three days! Save yourself if you are God's Son! Come on down from the cross!'

In the same way the chief priests and the teachers of the Law and the elders jeered at him:

'He saved others, but he cannot save himself! Isn't he the king of Israel? If he comes down off the cross now, we will believe in him! He trusts in God and claims to be God's Son. Well, then, let us see if God wants to save him now!'

Even the bandits who had been crucified with him insulted him in the same way.

At noon the whole country was covered with darkness, which lasted for three hours. At about three o'clock Jesus cried out with a loud shout,

'Eli, Eli, lema sabachthani?' which means, 'My God, my God, why did you abandon me?'

Some of the people standing there heard him and said, 'He is calling for Elijah!' One of them ran up at once, took a sponge, soaked it in cheap wine, put it on the end of a stick, and tried to make him drink it. But the others said, 'Wait, let us see if Elijah is coming to save him!' Jesus again gave a loud cry and breathed his last.

Then the curtain hanging in the Temple was torn in two from top to bottom.

The earth shook, the rocks split apart,

the graves broke open,

and many of God's people who had died were raised to life.

They left the graves, and after Jesus rose from death, they went into the Holy City, where many people saw them.

When the army officer and the soldiers with him who were watching Jesus saw the earthquake and everything else that happened, they were terrified and said,

'He really was the Son of God!'

Shocking! I don't know why God doesn't do something about the mess we're all in!

JESUS MURDERED

The reason

A talk & stories
5 mins

Using the following suggestions explain to the group the reason why Jesus had to die.

1. Start by referring back to the conclusions of meeting two when you discovered that we were made by God 'in his image' to be his friends, but have all turned away from him. Ask the group if they can remember what they thought God should do about the sin in each one of us; what did they write on their postcards? Make the point that we do deserve to be punished for rejecting God and causing others pain. If we don't want anything to do with God why should he want anything to do with us?

2. Go on to explain that, extraordinarily, God still loves us! He became a human being in Jesus to show us that he still wants to be friends.

3. Because God is totally fair and just (remember meeting one) he can't just say, 'Oh well, never mind. Let's all try again!' God's justice demands that our sin is punished. If it didn't then how would all the victims of crime, torture or murder feel if God just said to their persecutors, 'There, there, never mind'? It is not just a question of major sins being punished: all sin is serious to God and the punishment has to be taken.

4. The point about the death of Jesus is that he is taking the punishment that we deserve. It sounds crazy but it is true. When Jesus died on the cross he was taking the rap that you and I deserve for rejecting God. (Use one or all of the following examples to illustrate what it means for someone to die in another's place. If possible produce a visual aid for each; for example, a toy gun, bus or fluffy chick.)

The concentration camp

In a certain concentration camp during the Second World War, Nazi guards singled out a number of prisoners to be executed. Among their number was a young mother. An old priest was watching what was going on and when he saw the woman and thought of her children he stepped forward and begged the guards to let him take her place. 'I'm near the end of my life,' he said, 'whereas this woman is only beginning hers. She has children who need her. If someone has to die it would be better if it were me'. His offer was accepted.

The bus driver's son

One evening in late summer the local bus driver was returning home to the mountain village where he lived. He was travelling at some speed down the precipitous mountain road to the village. Suddenly, on turning a bend, he saw a little boy playing in the middle of the road. He could not stop the bus in time and had to make an instant decision. Either he could take the bus off the road and over the precipice and save the child, or save the passengers by running down the little boy. He ran the child down, stopped the bus, got out and picked up the dead boy, who was his only son.

Ten fluffy chicks

When hay barns catch fire they go up in flames in minutes. While searching through the smouldering remains of one such barn a farmer came across a dead mother hen lying on her nest with her wings spread out. When he picked her up he found underneath a brood of ten fluffy chicks alive and well, saved by the mother hen's sacrifice.

The Hot Seat

Interrogation time
4 mins

Set up the Hot Seat, switch on the light and play the Hot Seat theme music. Introduce the leader under the spotlight and explain that the group can ask them anything they like about their experience and understanding of the death of Jesus. Here are a couple of questions you may like to use to set the ball rolling:

● *How does the death of a man 2,000 years ago make a difference to you today?*
● *Do you feel responsible for the death of Jesus?*

Smash 'n' Grab

Getting the point
2 mins

Set up the Smash 'n' Grab screen and let them have their weekly chat. Remember what you see on the screen is what the group will see, so make it clear and simple.

Grab:	Hi, Smash! *(wave)*
Smash:	Hi-ya, Grab! *(shake hands)* 'Ow ya doin', mate?
Grab:	No too bad, thanks. *(thumbs up)*
Smash:	'Ave ya got the point, then?
Grab:	The point of what? *(palm up)*
Smash:	The point of the meetin'.
Grab:	Na, can't see it, mate. *(palm down)*
Smash:	*(pointing)* Well, the point is that Jesus died to take the punishment that we deserved for turning our backs on God.
Grab:	Oh right! Gotcha. Because of the death of Jesus we can be friends with God again. I see it now. *(Smash paper and grab point.)* I've got the point!
Smash:	You've got it, mate. You've got the point! *(thumbs up)*

Any answers

Qs & As
2 mins

Answer any questions put in the box at the last meeting. If you haven't had any yet perhaps you could plant one so that people get the idea. Take a look at page 115 for some suggestions.

Activities

Who am I?

Get everyone sitting in a circle. Write out the following names on separate sticky labels and stick one on each person's forehead. (Make sure there are no mirrors in the room.) Explain that each person is one of the characters mentioned in the death of Jesus reading. They have to work out who they are by taking it in turn to ask questions that can only be answered 'yes' or 'no'. For example, 'Was I present at the crucifixion?' If it takes more than three or four guesses, start giving clues. If you have more than eleven members, simply repeat some of the labels.

- Pilate
- Barabbas
- Simon of Cyrene
- Passers by
- Jesus
- Pilate's wife
- The thief on the cross
- Army Officer
- Crowds
- Roman soldier
- Chief Priests

The facts of the matter

Hand out copies of the worksheet and read the account of Jesus' trial and execution together. Ask each person to read the part of the person whose name is on their forehead. The passage in the worksheets has been divided up into chunks to be read by each character like this:

Pilate's wife *While Pilate was sitting in the judgement hall, his wife sent him a message: 'Have nothing to do with that innocent man, because in a dream last night I suffered much on account of him.'*

Chief Priest *The chief priests and the elders persuaded the crowd to ask Pilate to set Barabbas free and have Jesus put to death.*

Pilate *But Pilate asked the crowd, 'Which one of these two do you want me to set free for you?'*

Crowd *'BARABBAS!'*

If possible play the backing track used in the presentations section as you read. If you have less than eleven people in the group arrange for as many people as is necessary to read two parts. Once you have completed the reading take a wooden spoon and interview each character about their experience of the events. Ask them to explain what happened and how they feel about it. Will they sleep more or less easy in their beds tonight?

The death of Jesus?

Ask the group members to complete the 'Ponder this' questions on the sheet about their understanding of the death of Jesus.

- *What does the death of Jesus mean to you?*
- *What would you like to ask Jesus about his death?.*

Discussion
5 mins

The illustrations

Refer back to the three stories that shed light on the meaning of the death of Jesus. Perhaps you could get members of the group to re-tell them in their own words. This will help you to see how much they have understood. Discuss them together and ask the group how these stories help them understand the meaning of Jesus' death.

Testimony
2 mins

My story

Explain to the group what the death of Jesus means to you personally and how it has affected your life. Try and make this as clear, brief and honest as possible.

The crunch
2 mins

Taking stock

Ask the group members to read the statements under the 'Taking stock' heading in their worksheets and indicate how much they agree or disagree with each by putting a cross somewhere on the line between the two extremes.

1. Jesus was a great teacher but not the Son of God.

strongly agree ———————————————————— strongly disagree

2. Jesus' death was a tragic mistake.

strongly agree ———————————————————— strongly disagree

3. Jesus' death was something to do with me.

strongly agree ———————————————————— strongly disagree

4. When Jesus died he was taking the punishment for my sin.

strongly agree ———————————————————— strongly disagree

Presentations 2

Join back together for the last 15 minutes and explore the fantastic fact of the resurrection.

Resurrection account
3 mins

The facts of the matter

Explain to the group that the death of Jesus wasn't the end of the story. Two days later something very strange happened. Read to the group John's account of the resurrection (John 20:1–18), using the same style as before. Play the resurrection backing track on the audio cassette as you read.

Early on Sunday morning, while it was still dark, Mary Magdalene went to the tomb and saw that the stone had been taken away from the entrance.

She went running to Simon Peter and the other disciple, whom Jesus loved, and told them, 'They have taken the Lord from the tomb, and we don't know where they have put him!'

Then Peter and the other disciple went to the tomb. The two of them were running, but the other disciple ran faster than Peter and reached the tomb first. He bent over and saw the linen wrappings, but he did not go in.

Behind him came Simon Peter, and he went straight into the tomb. He saw the linen wrappings lying there and the cloth which had been round Jesus' head. It was not lying with the linen wrappings but was rolled up by itself.

Then the other disciple, who had reached the tomb first, also went in; he saw and believed. (They still did not understand the scripture which said that he must rise from death.) Then the disciples went back home.

Mary stood crying outside the tomb. While she was still crying, she bent over and looked in the tomb and saw two angels there dressed in white, sitting where the body of Jesus had been, one at the head and the other at the feet.

'Woman, why are you crying?' they asked her.

She answered, "They have taken my Lord away, and I do not know where they have put him!" Then she turned round and saw Jesus standing there; but she did not know that it was Jesus.

'Woman, why are you crying?' Jesus asked her. 'Who is it that you are looking for?'

She thought he was the gardener, so she said to him, 'If you took him away, sir, tell me where you have put him, and I will go and get him.'

Jesus said to her, 'Mary!'

She turned towards him and said, 'Teacher'.

'Do not hold on to me,' Jesus told her, 'because I have not yet gone back up to the Father. But go to my brothers and tell them that I am returning to him who is my Father and their Father, my God and their God.'

So Mary Magdalene went and told the disciples that she had seen the Lord and related to them what he had told her.

Evidence please

A sketch
2 mins

This sketch is a good way of getting across some of the evidence for the resurrection of Jesus. It is a phone conversation between the editor of a Jerusalem newspaper and one of his crack reporters. You only need one actor and a telephone. Phone ringing sound effects are on the audio cassette. (If you place the script by the phone you can discreetly read it. Remember to listen to what Sidney is saying on the other end of the line before replying!)

...I don't deal with UFO stories, you understand? Now goodbye.
  (phone rings)
...Hello, Jerusalem Journal, editor speaking.
...Sidney, hello. What's new?
...Of course I know abut the Jesus execution. It made the front page, remember?
...By the what? The tomb? What are you doing there?
...Oh, I see. So someone stole the body. Well, who was it?
...You're paid to know! Who have you asked?
...Isn't he the guy whose tomb it is?
...So what did he say?
...Women? What women?

...What did they say?

...And you believe that? About angels? Come on, Sidney!

...Well, to me it's obvious. They took the body themselves.

...The women, the disciples, whatever.

...So, they got some friends to help.

...Stone. What kind of stone?

...So what did the guards say?

...Eight Roman soldiers falling asleep on guard duty? They'd have been executed for that. Wake up Sidney. They were bribed.

...Yes, by this guy's disciples.

...OK, OK, I wasn't thinking. I suppose they wouldn't have taken it from Jews. So it was an inside job.

...OK, maybe not, but listen, Sidney, what are you trying to say here? Are you trying to tell me this Jesus guy's alive?

...Come on, Sidney, he was flogged, whipped, bashed about the head, crucified, then stabbed in the side. I mean, these army blokes don't muck about! On top of that he was starved from Thursday night. It would take more that the kiss of life to bring him back!

...This sounds awfully like some religious myth, Sidney.

...So people have seen him have they?

...So did anyone at the meal have a camera?

...And then what? Vanished?

...Without photos this story's dead. It's dead anyway, Sidney. People are tired of religious maniacs and their claims.

...Sidney, what are you, some kind of nut?

...Listen, I've been editor of this paper for fifteen years, and if there's one thing I've learnt in all that time, it's this—true stories last, they stick around. Sidney, tell me honestly, this Jesus stuff, do you think they will still be talking about it in a year's time?

Marcus Idle

The implications

The point
1 min

Ask one of the leaders or even an older member of the group to briefly share what the resurrection means to them. Perhaps they could work round the point that when God raised Jesus from the dead he showed that he accepted Jesus' death in our place. Because of the resurrection we can know that God's rescue plan for the human race has worked. Hurraaay! St Paul put it like this: 'Because of our sins Jesus was handed over to die, and he was raised to life in order to put us right with God' (Romans 4:25).

Getting to Grips with
Becoming a Christian

The Aim: To help each member of the group take a step forward in their relationship with Jesus.

The Lightning Bolt: Romans 3:23–26.
God's free gift.

Equipment Checklist

PRESENTATIONS
- ❏ theme music
- ❏ Question Mark outfit
- ❏ props for quiz show recap
- ❏ free gift sketch & talk props
- ❏ Hot Seat, light & theme tune
- ❏ Smash 'n' Grab kit
- ❏ paper slips & pens
- ❏ questions box

ACTIVITIES
- ❏ worksheets & pens
- ❏ pins & words of verse on paper
- ❏ Agony Aunt letters & writing paper
- ❏ small wrapped present

Letter to leaders

This meeting is all about helping the young people in your group to actively take a step forward in their relationship with Jesus. For some this will mean taking the plunge and becoming Christians. This can be quite a definite decision. Jane became a Christian when she was fifteen. A friend from school took her to a Christian meeting where she heard the good news about Jesus clearly explained, accepted it for herself and was amazed that no one had ever told her about it before.

Though the members of your group might not have such a dramatic response to the gospel it is important to offer them the opportunity to make a decision to accept it for themselves. Some will be ready to do this but others won't. Either way, offering them the opportunity to decide helps each person work out where they stand with God and see what they need to do to take a step closer to him.

- *How did you come to start following Jesus? Try explaining it out loud in less than two minutes. Why not ask a friend to listen to your story and help you make it clearer. Alternatively, tape-record your explanation and play it back to yourself.*

- *Pray that each member of the group will take a step towards God whether by airing their questions, learning how to help others to follow Jesus, or actually making that decision for themselves.*

Presentations

 **Quiz show**

A recap
8 mins

Have the theme music playing as the group arrives and give them a warm welcome. Start by running a quick quiz show to recap on the lessons of the last four meetings. Split four or six volunteers into two competing teams, sit them at the front and ask them the following questions. Try and keep it moving and don't let it drag on.

1. Getting to Grips with God
- Display a selection photographs of animals and plants, etc. Ask the teams to explain what light they shed on the question of God's existence. See pages 26 and 27.
- Give each team thirty seconds to make a list of as many 'God words' as they can. See page 32.

2. Getting to Grips with Life
- Give each team a red and green card and ask them to explain what they tell us about the meaning of life. See pages 35 and 36. Human beings were created by God in his image to be like him.
- Then ask them what Fred the Funky Chicken discovered. See pages 36 and 37.

3. Getting to Grips with Jesus
- Get the teams to compete in a verbal tennis match. Explain that in meeting three you investigated Jesus' parables, miracles, claims and personal details (from birth to death). Select one of these categories (e.g. parables) and get the two teams to take it in turns to name a parable until one team can't think of any more. The other team scores each time this happens. Repeat this game with the other three categories.

4. Getting to Grips with the Rescue
- Produce a picture of a bus, hen and gun and ask the two teams to explain what each tells us about God's response to the mess our lives are in. See pages 53 and 54.

 Leading questions

Introduction
1 min

Very briefly sum up the point of the last four meetings:

- *We have examined the evidence for God's existence and what we can know about him.*
- *We've seen that he created us to be his friends but that we have turned away from him.*
- *We've investigated his invasion into human history in the person of Jesus.*
- *We've seen that his death and resurrection have made it possible for our friendship with God to be repaired.*

Conclude by explaining that the crunch comes when we decide how we will respond to God's offer of forgiveness. In meeting five you will be getting to grips with becoming a Christian and grappling with such questions as (shouted out by Question Mark):

- *How do I become a Christian?*
- *How do I know if I'm one already?*
- *How do I know **if** I'm ready?*
- *What will it cost?*
- *And what will happen next?*

Thank Mark for his questions and conclude by saying that becoming a Christian is simply a matter of accepting God's wonderful free gift.

A word about free gifts

A sketch
3 mins

This is a brief sketch on the subject of free gifts. A leader enters holding a small plastic model (e.g. fluorescent yellow slug) and has a conversation along the following lines with the group.

Leader: *Hey. You'll never guess what I found in my cereal this morning... yes, a free fluorescent yellow rubber slug! I mean what is the point of that?! It's just a stupid gimmick to get kids to make their parents buy sugar frosted flakes of corn. It's a con—a total con.*

(Leaflet comes through the letter box) That'll be the post... Hmm. (Opens letter) Oh no, I don't believe it! Not another free gift offer... Oh gosh, listen to this one, 'Dear Sir/Madam, you have been especially selected because of your extraordinary good looks and up-market address to be the proud recipient of a magnificent pair of fluffy dice to hang from your car's rear-view mirror. All you have to do is subscribe to the Motor Mechanics Monthly Magazine for the next five years and these remarkable dice will be yours absolutely free!' Well, isn't that kind of them! (Screws up letter and bins it)

(Phone rings) Hello... yes... no really, I'm not interested... I've told you I'm not interested... Look, I do not want to take out insurance against the risk of my children absconding to Venezuela with the family pet... NO! Not even if I do get a FREE A to Z of Venezuelan wild life. Do I make myself clear! (Slams phone down)

(Door bell rings) Oh, good grief! Who can this be? (Answers door)

Salesperson: *Good morning, Sir/Madam. I'm calling on behalf of Smash and Fix Double Glazing Specialists. We're currently running a special promotion. Your beautiful house has been individually selected for our 10% off complete double glazing service. If you agree to re-glaze with Smash and Fix Double Glazing Specialists we will throw in a FREE, yes FREE bottle of Smash and Fix Window Cleaning Fluid. Surely an offer you can't refuse!*

Leader: *(To salesperson) No, NO! no no no, NO NO, no No NO NO NO NO **NO!** (Slams door and then to audience) Free gifts—I've just had it up to here! (Exits, shaking head)*

God's free gift

A gift worth having
3 mins

Before the meeting write out Romans 3:24 on a piece of paper, put it in a box and wrap it up with fancy paper and a bow. Explain that though free gifts are often a big con there is one free gift that is rather different. It is a free gift from God. Ask someone to unwrap the parcel and read what they find inside, *'By the free gift of God's grace all are put right with him through Christ Jesus, who sets them free.'* Explain that God's FREE GIFT to us is his loving goodness that frees us from our sin and puts us right with him.

Though we have messed up our lives and turned our backs on God, he wants us to be his friends again. His son Jesus has made it possible for us to be put right with God by taking the blame for our sin on the cross (as we saw last week). The ultimate free gift of being put right with God is there for the taking. Go on to talk briefly (1–2 minutes) about what God's free gift means to you.

How do I become a Christian?

The steps
2 mins

Explain to the group how to accept God's free gift and become a Christian.

- **A Christian is someone who has realized that they are not very good at being 'in charge' of their life and living it in a way that pleases God.** Think back to meeting two when you discovered that we all do so much that is wrong. Doing what we want comes more easily than doing what we know we should. A Christian is someone who realises this and has asked God to forgive them. God will **always** forgive us when we come to him and say sorry, no matter how bad we are.

- **A Christian is someone who has asked God to be 'in charge' of their life and help them run it in the way he wants.** Imagine your life is a football or netball team. When you were the captain things weren't too hot; you might have won the odd game but you lost many more and got quite a few red and yellow cards for bad behaviour. Now there's a new captain 'in charge' of the team, changes have to be made. You'll have to start training harder, you'll have to follow a new game-plan, you'll have to be loyal to the new captain and do what he or she says. Your team won't change its name or its outfit but the new captain will want other things changed. It's just like that with God. Once he is 'in charge' of your life he'll need to start making changes too. You won't change your name or your looks but the new captain will want to get you living in a way that pleases him.

So becoming a Christian is simply a case of realizing that you're not too good at running your life in the way that God wants and asking him to forgive you and be 'in charge' of your life from now on. Hand out the worksheets and pens and ask the group to jot down at the bottom of the 'What is a Christian?' section anything that is not clear about what you have just said. Perhaps they could put these queries to the leader on the Hot Seat.

The Hot Seat

Interrogation time
4 mins

Set up the spotlight and Hot Seat and play the Hot Seat theme music. Explain to the group that they can now ask the leader on the Hot Seat anything they like about how they became a Christian, why they are a Christian, and what being a Christian is like. It might help if you set the ball rolling. Here are a couple of questions you could ask:

● *How did you realize that you are not good at running your life in the way God wants?*
● *When you asked God to be 'in charge' of your life what difference did it make?*

Smash 'n' Grab

Getting the point
2 mins

Set up the Smash 'n' Grab screen and run a conversation along the following lines:

Grab: Hi, Smash! *(wave)*
Smash: Hi-ya, Grab! *(take five)* 'Ow ya doin', mate?
Grab: No too bad, thanks. *(thumbs up)*
Smash: 'Ave ya got the point then?
Grab: The point of what? *(palm up)*
Smash: The point of the meetin'.
Grab: Na, can't see it, mate. *(palm down)*
Smash: *(pointing)* Well, the point is that we humans are no good at being in charge of our lives and the only way round it is to ask God to be 'in charge'. That's what becoming a Christian is.
Grab: Well, well well… You know, I've had this funny feeling that something's not been right with my life for a few years now, but couldn't put my finger on it. Now you've pointed it out I can see I do need God's help with living. Yea, I can see it now *(smash paper and grab point)*. I've got the point!
Smash: You've got it mate. You've got the point! *(thumbs up)*

So where do you stand?

Decision time
3 mins

Ask each member of the group to look through the five positions under the 'Where do you stand?' heading in the worksheets. Run through them explaining what each one means and ask them to tick the one that best sums up their position. Do reassure them that you really don't mind which box they tick so long as they are being honest with themselves and with God.

1. ☐ *I have realized that I'm not good at running my life and have asked God to be 'in charge'. I'm still not perfect and I don't understand it all, but I am a Christian.*

2. ☐ *I'm not sure if I've asked God to be in charge of my life or not. I don't know if I'm a Christian.*

3. ☐ *I think I understand what becoming a Christian would mean, but I'm not ready to ask God to be 'in charge' of my life just yet.*

4. ☐ *I find this all a bit confusing and don't really know what to think.*

5. ☐ *I realize that I'm not good at running my life in a way that pleases God. I'm really sorry about this and would like to ask God to be 'in charge' of my life from now on.*

Explain to the group that in order to be of most help to them you would like to split them into groups in which everyone is at the same stage. Hand out slips of paper and ask each person to jot down their name and the number of the box they ticked. Collect these in and arrange them into the following three groups.

Activity group 1
People who have ticked box 1 or 2 and who are either Christians already or not sure.

Activity group 2
People who have ticked boxes 3 or 4 and who are confused or not ready.

Activity group 3
People who have ticked box 5 and would like to become Christians.

If you have any older group members who are Christians it would be a good idea to put one or two of them into each group as helpers. The younger group members will benefit from hearing about the experiences of people nearer their age. I have suggested a range of different activities appropriate for each of the three activity groups.

Any answers

Qs & As
2 mins

Answer any questions in the questions box from last week while someone works out the new groups. Then read out the list of new groups and where they are meeting.

Activity group 1

Introductions

My story
5 mins

Start off by asking everyone to introduce themselves. Perhaps they could do it by combining their name with their favourite food. For example, Nick Chocolate Jones, or Jane Cheese Blazeby. Ask if anyone would like to have a go at remembering everyone's 'names'. Then ask each person to explain which box they ticked and why. Perhaps those who have ticked Box 1 could explain how and when they came to ask Jesus to be 'in charge' of their lives. This should help those who ticked Box 2 to be more sure one way or the other. You will probably find that most of the 'not sures' are Christians but just aren't sure that they are. If you tell your story first it will help create an open and honest atmosphere.

God's free gift

Write out the words of Romans 3:24 on separate pieces of paper. If you have ten people in your group you will need to write them on ten pieces of paper (see example below). Pin one piece of paper on each person's back and ask them to sort themselves into the right order. Finish by saying the verse together a few times.

BY THE—FREE GIFT—OF GOD'S—GRACE ALL—ARE PUT—RIGHT WITH HIM THROUGH—CHRIST JESUS—WHO SETS—THEM FREE.

Being sure

**Agony aunts
and uncles**
15 mins

This is an exercise to help the group think about what it means to be a Christian. Explain that you have a selection of problem page letters from anxious Christians that you would like them to try and answer, either working on their own or in pairs. Photocopy the letters on page 66, cut them up and hand them out along with some paper on which they can write a reply. When they have completed their replies join back together and discuss. You may find some helpful clues in the answer to the question 'How do I know if I'm a Christian?' on page 119.

Any questions

A discussion
5 mins

Give the group the chance to talk about some of the things they find hard about being a Christian or about the Christian faith. To get the discussion going perhaps you could ask them what they might write to a Christian agony aunt or uncle about. Perhaps they could put these questions in the questions box.

Thank you God

Pray together
4 mins

Spend some time praying together. Encourage each group member to write a prayer on the worksheet thanking God for his wonderful free gift of forgiveness and love. Then pass a small wrapped parcel (symbolizing God's free gift) round the group and explain that when it gets to them that is their turn to pray their prayer, either out loud or silently.

Taking stock

The crunch
2 mins

Conclude by asking the group to fill in the 'Taking stock' section of their worksheets. Discuss what they have written together if appropriate. The questions are:

- *What has been the crunch for you in this meeting?*
- *What will you do about it?*

Dear Andrew,

You know how Christians say that God forgives us when we say sorry for the wrong things we've done? Well, I've said sorry over and over again but I don't feel forgiven. What am I doing wrong? Please write soon.

Worried of Wells

Dear Amanda,

I've always believed in God and gone to church and tried to pray, but I find it so hard and God seems a million miles away. What's wrong with me, or what am I doing wrong? Please tell me, or I feel I'll give up all together.

Despairing of Dungeness

Dear Albert,

Hello. I asked Jesus to be in charge of my life about a year ago and I am trying to be a good Christian. But I keep doing things that I know are wrong, like swearing and hitting my brother. Why isn't it working? Please help.

Struggling of Slough

Dear Angela,

I asked Jesus to be in charge of my life last summer on a Christian camp. At first it was great and I was pleased to be friends with God, but now I don't feel any different and I don't think I'm a real Christian any more. Please help.

Doubting of Doncaster

Dear Arthur,

I've been thinking about asking Jesus to be in charge of my life, but I'm worried that he'll ask me to do something I don't want to do, like be a missionary. Will he do that and is it OK to ask him to be only half in charge of my life?

Anxious of Ashford

Dear Annabell,

I hope you don't mind me writing. The thing is that I'd quite like to be a Christian. I'm sure it's the right thing to do. My only worry is that my friends will think I'm weird and will laugh at me. And what if they ask me a question I can't answer?

Nervous of Newcastle

Activity group 2

 ## Introductions

My story
5 mins

Start off by asking everyone to introduce themselves. Perhaps they could do it by combining their name with their favourite food. For example, Nick Chocolate Jones, or Jane Cheese Blazeby. Then ask if anyone would like to have a go at remembering everyone's 'names'.

Then ask each person to explain which box they ticked and why. This should get them talking about where they stand and bring up the questions or worries that they have. Discussion of these may well take up most of the group time. Below are a couple of activities that may help them think the issues through more thoroughly.

 ## My question list

Questions to be
answered
5 mins

Ask the group members to make a list on the worksheet of all the questions they have about the Christian faith. Read through these together and discuss. Encourage them to hang on to their list and tick off the questions as and when they get good answers. Suggest that they start their quest for answers by writing out the most pressing question and putting it in the questions box there and then.

 ## Pros & cons

In the balance
5 mins

Ask each person to make a list of the pros and cons of becoming a Christian on the scales on the worksheet. Once they have done this ask each person to run through the items on their lists and how they weigh up. If possible get hold of some balancing scales (labelled PROS one side and CONS the other) so that each person can use them as they explain how the two sides of the argument weigh up for them. Do challenge them to follow up their conclusions with appropriate action.

 ## Other activities

Extras
8 mins

If there is time, do the 'God's free gift' activity (a look at Romans 3:24) described in the outline for Activity group 1 and conclude by filling in the 'Taking stock' section of the worksheet.

Activity group 3

Introductions

My story
5 mins

Start off by asking everyone to introduce themselves by combining their name with their favourite food. E.g. Nick Chocolate Jones, or Jane Cheese Blazeby.

Then ask each person to explain why they ticked Box 5. This will help you to see how well they understand all that you have talked about. Explain again the two steps involved in becoming a Christian and accepting God's free gift. Let the group members ask any questions they still have. If you are satisfied that they know what is involved in becoming a follower of Jesus and that that is what they want to do, suggest that you all pray together.

Taking the plunge

Praying together
3 mins

Ask each person to write a prayer on their worksheet asking God to forgive them for when they have not lived their life very well in the past and to be 'in charge' of their life from now on. Pass a small wrapped parcel (symbolizing God's free gift) round the group and explain that when it gets to them it is their turn to pray their prayer either silently or out loud. Once the parcel has been round the group pray for each group member in turn.

Then welcome them into God's family. Explain that today is the first day of their new life with God and that in the next five *Getting to Grips with God* meetings you will be exploring the everyday issues of following Jesus. If appropriate do let them know that they can always come to you if they ever need help or have questions they want answered. I'm sure they would appreciate it if you wrote them an encouraging letter in the week as well.

Tell a friend

A task
1 min

Explain that when someone becomes a Christian it is always a good idea if they tell a friend what they have done. Ask them to jot down in the space provided under the 'What should I do?' heading on the worksheets the name of a Christian they would like to tell.

Other activities

Extras
8 mins

If there is time finish by doing the 'God's free gift' activity (a look at Romans 3:24) described in the outline for Activity group 1 and then the 'Taking stock' section of the worksheets.

Part 2

Jesus said,
'Love the Lord your God with all your heart,
with all your soul, and with all your mind
and love your neighbour as you love yourself.'

Matthew 22:37–39

In the remaining five *Getting to Grips with God* meetings
we will be grappling with how we can do just that.

Getting to Grips
with Prayer

The Aim: To see how God is always with us and how we can talk to him about anything.

The Lightning Bolt: Matthew 6:5–15.
Jesus on prayer.

Equipment Checklist

PRESENTATIONS
❏ theme music
❏ Question Mark outfit
❏ acorn or seed
❏ rap backing tape
❏ Lord's prayer sketch props
❏ 10 prayer objects
❏ Hot Seat, light & theme music
❏ Smash 'n' Grab kit
❏ questions box

ACTIVITIES
❏ worksheets & pens
❏ props for lightning sketches
❏ sheets of A4 plain paper
❏ magazines

Letter to leaders

No doubt you have heard the overworked phrase 'Prayer changes things'. Well, it's actually true. More importantly prayer is the principal means through which God changes *us*. When we pray we change. If, for example, you were praying for a friend or relative who is feeling lonely, your prayer might inspire you to go and visit them. On a broader level it is impossible really to pray that God's will is done in your life without being ready to change the way you behave. In these last five *Getting to Grips with God* meetings we will discover that the principal change God wants to make in our lives is that we love him and our neighbours more completely.

Prayer is the main business of the Christian's life and all who have walked closely with God have, like Jesus, made it an absolute priority. I pray that, in this meeting, you would grow in your love for God through rediscovering the wonder of life-changing prayer.

● **Have you ever been changed because you've been praying?**

● **What one thing can you do this week to make your prayer life more effective? Perhaps you could start praying regularly with a friend. Once a week for five minutes would be a good start.**

Presentations

 ## *A lesson in growing*

**Welcome and
introduction
2 min**

Play the theme music as the group arrives and give them a very warm welcome. Start off by explaining that whichever box they ticked last week—whether they asked Jesus to be in charge of their life, still had questions, or were already following him—there is one important thing that you want them to know, and it's this:

Being a Christian is rather like being a tree. If a tree is to stay alive it has to keep growing day by day. So do Christians. (*Hold up an acorn or a seed*.) When you plant an acorn, a mature, fully grown tree doesn't suddenly explode out of the ground. The seed very slowly grows into a sapling and eventually years later becomes a mature tree. We are to grow like that as Christians, slowly becoming more like Jesus over the years. You don't suddenly become a mini-Jesus the moment you ask him to be 'in charge' of your life. That's simply the first step in a life-time of growth. So, whether you are a seed lying dormant underground, or a very young shoot, or a little sapling, or even a young tree, your goal is the same: to grow a little bit more each day.

This is what the last five *Getting to Grips with God* meetings will help your group members to do. You will start by getting to grips with prayer and grappling with such questions as (shouted out by Question Mark):

- *Can I really talk to God?*
- *Will he talk to me?*
- *How should I do it?*
- *Where should I do it?*
- *How do I know if he's listening?*

 ## *Teach us to pray*

**Jesus on
prayer
2 mins**

This poem or rap is a version of Matthew 6:5–15. Either read it to the group or perform it as a rap using the backing track on the audio cassette. At the end of each verse a few disciples should respond with the disciple refrain. Introduce it by saying that one day Jesus' disciples asked him to teach them to pray. This illustrates how he responded:

Right lads, Jesus started, if you want to learn to pray
Gather round and listen: I will show you the best way
And give you an outline of the kind of things to say
Disciple refrain . . . *the kind of things to say*

The first point to make is that prayer's a private matter
You and God alone having a good natter
So do it somewhere quiet away from noise and clatter
Disciple refrain . . . *away from noise and clatter*

Don't make your prayers impressive—a long and fancy speech
That doesn't make them better or more likely God to reach
Understand what I'm saying? The point I'm trying to teach?
Disciple refrain . . . *not a long and fancy speech*

The third point to make is that God knows what you mean
Everything that you need he's already seen
He's more in touch with you than you have ever been
Disciple refrain . . . so God knows what we mean

Now I'm giving you a prayer to use every single day
Take it as an outline of the kind of things to say
Or use it as a prayer when you simply want to pray
Disciple refrain . . . a prayer for every single day

Our Father in heaven, may your holy name be praised
(When you realise God's your dad it's natural to be fazed
And want his name respected everywhere and always)
Disciple refrain . . . may your holy name be praised

May your kingdom come and your will be done in me
(If you want to live for God then this bit is the key
God's love will shine in you for everyone to see)
Disciple refrain . . . may your will be done in me

Then ask God to give you just the food and clothes you need
It's not good to go hungry or to live in greed
Commit your needs to him and your family he will feed
Disciple refrain . . . just the food and clothes we need

Forgive us our sins as we forgive sins against us
(Sin is like a massive boil, swollen full of pus
The only way to lance it is to seek God's forgiveness)
Disciple refrain . . . is to seek God's forgiveness

Keep us safe from the grips of the evil one
(Steer clear from trouble, I don't mean don't have fun—
Just don't do anything that you don't think I'd have done)
Disciple refrain . . . keep us safe from temptation

I think that wraps it up—that's all I want to say
Above all please remember be honest when you pray
And make it something that you do every single day
Disciple refrain . . . we'll pray every single day

The Lord's Prayer

A bedroom sketch
4 mins

This is a simple sketch about someone praying the Lord's prayer and getting more than they bargained for. If you are running *Getting to Grips with God* in someone's home it would be great if you could lead everyone into the bedroom and get them sitting on the floor round the bed. Do make an effort to create a real bedtime atmosphere—pyjamas and all. The leader who is playing God should be concealed somewhere in the room, perhaps behind the curtains. If it is not possible to use a bedroom get hold of a bedside light and make the meeting room as bedroomy as possible.

Cast: GOD and YOUNG PERSON.

Enter young person. He or she gets ready for bed whilst talking to him/herself. Perhaps they could get into bed and then realize that they have forgotten to clean their teeth and say their prayers. They end up kneeling by the bed and start following the script below. This could be placed on the bed and discreetly read.

YP: Our Father in heaven . . .

God: Yes?

YP: *(looks around room slightly confused and then starts again.)* Our Father in heaven… *(looks up and listens)*

God: Yes. I **am** listening.

YP: *(looks confused and starts again.)* Our Father in heaven, hal-… *(pauses, looks suspiciously round room)*

God: Hallowed… Look, it's God here. Sorry to interrupt, but you did call.

YP: Eh?… Oh yes, I suppose I did. But I wasn't really expecting any… er… what do I say now?

God: I don't mind. Why don't you carry on with what you were saying?

YP: OK. *(deep breath)* Hallowed be your name… *(pause)*

God: What's the matter?

YP: I'm scared. I'm not used to talking to… to God, and having you in my room. I kind of feel really tiny. Like I don't deserve to have you listening to me…

God: Well, that's good. That's because you're beginning to realize who you're talking to. That's what 'hallowed be your name' means.

YP: Really? Well, hallowed be your name… Shall I carry on?… OK, your kingdom come. Your will be done on earth as it is in heaven.

God: Look Jon *(YP's name)*. My kingdom **is** on its way, but I need your help if my will is to be done on earth.

YP: My help?… I don't understand.

God: Well, it's like this. My will is only going to be done on earth if individuals like you do it in their lives. Do you know what my will for you is?

YP: I don't think so.

God: Well, it is for you to love me with your whole heart and love your neighbour as much as you love yourself.

YP: *(pause)* That sounds quite a tall order… Well, I'll try, but I think you're going to have to help me.

God: No problem!

YP: OK. Give us today our daily bread… Haven't I said that already?

God: Yes you have in a funny kind of way. I'll help you and provide for all your needs, whatever they are. *(pause)* Anyway, you were saying… *(pause)* What's the matter?

YP: I'm not sure I can say this next bit.

God: Why not? You've said it before.

YP: Yes, but it's different with you here.

God: Shall I go then?

YP: No! Don't go… I'll try. *(fast)* Forgive us our sins as we forgive those who sin against us.

God: What about Pete?

YP: *(sigh)* I knew you'd drag him into it and I know what you're going to say—you're going to tell me to forgive him. But I can't. You don't know what he's done to me! He's been ruining my life and he's going to pay for it!

God: I can't forgive you if you can't forgive Pete.

YP: Oh God! I wasn't expecting all this hassle. I was just praying and then you show up and now I'm really confused. *(sigh)* Oh, I don't know! You can't expect me just to let him get away with it… can you?… You know I hate his guts and wish he'd go and take a trip under a... Look God, I think you're going to have to help me forgive him. I suppose it can't be that nice for him being that messed up inside... and I don't like it that much either. I'm sorry. Maybe you could give him some special attention. I'm sure that would help.

God: Maybe I will. And maybe you can help me...

YP: Mmm, maybe... Anyway, lead us not into temptation, but deliver... deliver us... from... from evil...

God: Well?

YP: I'm just thinking about what you might be thinking about. Tell me if I'm wrong, but you're thinking that I ought to start delivering myself from temptation and evil... Yes, I thought as much. So I ought to stop hanging around with those lads after school... it's looking for trouble... You know God, you sound a bit like my mum. Well, I get the point. I'll see what I can do. OK, shall I wind up now? For yours is the kingdom, the power and the glory, for ever and ever. Amen.

God: Thanks. I really appreciated that.

YP: Really! Well, it kind of means more when you're here.

God: But I'm always here. You just haven't noticed before.

YP: What?... That's awful! Well, I'm really sorry... You've been here all along and I never knew!...

God: Don't let it bother you. You've noticed now, and I'm pleased. Sleep well.

YP: Yeah, thanks. I suppose I'll see you in the morning.

(gets into bed and turns out the light)

Object hints

Prayer tips
5 mins

Get hold of the following ten objects or their equivalents and briefly explain what helpful hints they give us about prayer. If you want to make it more dramatic you could put them on a makeshift conveyor belt. (Wrap a long piece of material over and under a table and get someone just out of sight to pull the material towards them and feed it back under the table and round again. Objects placed on the table will then move with the fabric, conveyor-belt style.) If this is not possible why not phone a few of the leaders and young people the week before and ask each to explain one of the prayer objects?

Arrow

The arrow represents 'arrow prayers' This is simply a question of firing up prayers to God when you are out and about. As you travel to school on the bus perhaps you could imagine Jesus walking down the bus touching your friends on the shoulders and telling them that he loves them and wants to become part of their lives. If you hear a baby crying why not flash up a prayer for that family? When you pass a homeless person why not fire up a prayer for them?

Family photo

It's a good idea to pray for the members of your family. Why not find some family photos and pray for each person in them. Having something to focus your mind on as you pray can be very helpful.

Friendship bracelet (or other friendship object)

Find a Christian friend and get together each week for five minutes and pray for each other and the things that are on your minds.

Sorry dog (toy dog with a 'sorry' label tied to its collar)

It is important to say sorry to God when we hurt him. Say sorry to God just as you would to a friend or relative. Tell the group a 'saying sorry' story. Here's one about a little boy called Paul (now a vicar). Having been sent to his room for being naughty, little Paul summoned the family dog, attached a note of apology to its collar and sent him downstairs to his mum and dad. Better still think of one from your own life and change the object to tie in with it.

Television

Pray for world events. After you have watched the news on TV why not ask God to do something about the situations that have been reported?

Plasters

Use objects to focus your mind as you pray. If you know someone who is ill why not find a plaster and as you hold it pray for that person? If you have a friend who is depressed or who doesn't know Jesus try lighting a candle (be careful). As you look at it ask God to bring his light into their life or help them to 'see the light'.

Child's scribbles

God doesn't want fancy prayers, but just loves to hear from us however fumbling our prayers might sound. This true story makes the point nicely: While Mr and Mrs Smith were away at a conference they received a letter from their three children back home with Granny. They opened it with great excitement. First there was a letter from the oldest child aged eight—'Dear Mummy and Daddy, etc.' they were delighted. Then there was a rather tatty letter from Sam aged five—'dear mummy and daddy, i love you'; it brought tears to their eyes. But when they saw the piece of paper covered in multi-coloured scribbles from Marie aged two they were so delighted they both burst into tears.

Prayer rota

Put the people and things you want to pray for on a rota so you remember to pray for them each once a week. E.g. MONDAY: Mum, Granny, Hammie the hamster. TUESDAY: Dad, little bro., Liverpool FC, etc.

Prayer diary or letter

Write letters to God or keep a diary in which you write your prayers. Writing your prayers down really helps you keep them clear and specific and also means that you can look back and see how God has answered them. If you have ever done this give an example.

Prayer chair

Have a special place where you can go to pray, e.g. cupboard under the stairs or a special chair in your room. This helps you concentrate and keeps you away from distractions.

GOOD TO SEE
YOU JO.
HOW ARE YOU?

How long have
you got?

The Hot Seat

Interrogation time
4 mins

Set up the Hot Seat and light and play the Hot Seat theme tune. Let the group grill one of the leaders about their experience of prayer. (Perhaps you could invite a guest to come and be interrogated.) Set the ball rolling by asking questions of your own such as:

- *How do you know that you are not just talking to yourself when you pray?*
- *Give us an example of a time when God answered one of your prayers.*

Smash 'n' Grab

Getting the point
2 mins

Set up the Smash 'n' Grab screen and act out the following conversation.

Grab: Hi, Smash! *(wave)*
Smash: Hi-ya, Grab! *(take five or shake hands)* 'Ow ya doin', mate?
Grab: Not too bad, thanks. *(thumbs up)*
Smash: 'Ave ya got the point, then?
Grab: The point of what? *(palm up)*
Smash: The point of the meetin'
Grab: Na, can't see it, mate. *(palm down)*

Smash:	*(pointing)* Well, the point is we can talk to God anytime, anywhere. All he's worried about is that we're honest with him.
Grab:	Oh right! Gotcha. Prayer is talking with God; him and me, one to one. Now that you've pointed it out, I can see it. *(Smash and grab point)* I've got the point!
Smash:	You've got it, mate. You've got the point! *(thumbs up)*

Any answers

Qs & As
2 mins

Answer any questions placed in the box at the last meeting. Remember to try and keep your answers short and simple.

Activities

If possible stay in the same small groups as last meeting. This will enable you to tune what you do in the groups to the needs of your group members. If necessary carry on talking about the issues raised last meeting and deal with questions that have arisen since.

Introducing prayer

Prayer is . . .
5 mins

Welcome everyone to the small group and ask them how their week has been. Hand out the worksheets and ask them to complete the sentence 'Prayer is . . .' and discuss. Have a large piece of paper in the middle and jot down the recurring themes or words. Be ready to talk about your experience of prayer and your daily prayer routine. Also be prepared to answer any questions about prayer that the group may have.

Jesus on prayer

Lightning raps
& sketches
15 mins

Read Matthew 6:5–15 together in the worksheets. Below is a summary of the points that Jesus was making. Write out each on a separate slip of paper and put them in a hat. Split the group into pairs or threes and ask them to pick a piece of paper from the hat and write a verse of a rap exploring the point Jesus was making. Alternatively, they could knock together a sketch exploring what Jesus meant. If you do this, give them each three random props (e.g. banana, rope and cheque book) to work into their sketch. Then get back together and perform the raps or sketches in the correct order and discuss if appropriate.

- *Prayer is between you and God.*
- *Keep your prayers simple; there's no need to try and impress God.*
- *God understands what we mean and need even if we don't.*
- *Call God 'Father' and show reverence (respect) for who he is.*
- *Ask that God's kingdom would come and that his will would be done in your life.*
- *Ask God to provide what you need.*
- *Ask God to forgive the past (Note the condition that you forgive others).*
- *Ask God to keep you safe in the future.*

The handy hints

Memory test
5 mins

Ask the group to draw or list the ten prayer objects and jot down next to each the prayer hints that they give us. There is a space in the worksheets for them to do this. Then ask each member of the group to explain one of the prayer objects to the rest of the group.

Designer leaflets

Prayer information
12 mins

Hand out sheets of plain A4 paper and ask the group members to design a leaflet for new Christians giving essential information on the how, why, when, what, who, and where of prayer. Do encourage them to think of interesting ways of folding it and laying it out. While they are working on this you will have the opportunity to chat to them individually.

Pictured prayers

Praying together
5 mins

Hand out some magazines and ask each person to choose a photo that they can make into a prayer. These could be prayers of thanks for our world, prayers for people in the news, or prayers about anything else. They can either stick their photo on the worksheet or write their prayer on the photo. Explain that you are going to pass the small present used last week round the group. When it gets to them they can pray their prayer out loud or silently.

Taking stock

The crunch
3 mins

Ask everyone to fill in the 'Taking stock' section of the worksheet and decide on one way they will try and pray a little bit more in the week ahead. Perhaps they could share these with a partner.

Getting to Grips
with the Bible

The Aim: To discover that reading the Bible is an excellent way of getting to grips with God.

The Lightning Bolt: 2 Timothy 3:16.
All Scripture is inspired by God.

Equipment Checklist

PRESENTATIONS
- ❏ theme music
- ❏ Question Mark outfit
- ❏ buzzers & selection of books
- ❏ Bible advert backing track
- ❏ Hot Seat, light & theme music
- ❏ Smash 'n' Grab kit
- ❏ questions box

ACTIVITIES
- ❏ worksheets & pens
- ❏ pass the parcel & music
- ❏ Bibles
- ❏ copies of daily readings

Letter to leaders

All good friendships involve two-way communication and so should our friendship with God. We speak to him through prayer, and may experience him speaking to us through our conscience, our friends, or meeting with other believers. God has also given us a more concrete account of his message. The Bible contains God's words written down for us to digest at our leisure and he speaks through them. No doubt you have experienced verses 'jumping out at you' and telling you something you need to know.

God also speaks through the Bible in a perhaps more significant way. As you read and digest the scriptures over the years they become part of you. You absorb the words of God, the example of Jesus and the wisdom of his followers. Without realizing it, this changes you. It changes the way you think, and influences your decisions and behaviour. You begin to know the mind of God and 'think his thoughts after him'. This gradual process only happens when you regularly read and ponder the words of the Bible.

The habit of regular Bible reading is one we want to encourage in our young people. As with most aspects of Christian behaviour, a love for the Bible is caught not taught. Our young people will only grow up to desire to read the Bible if they see that desire in us. If they see that reading God's word makes a difference to us they'll catch the habit too.

- *How did you come to start reading the Bible? Who or what helped you most?*

- *Would you be happy if your group members read the Bible the same amount as you? What can you do about this?*

Presentations

 **Leading questions**

Welcome & introduction
1 min

Play the theme music as the group arrives and give them a warm welcome. Remind the group that being a Christian is all about loving God with all our heart, and loving our neighbours as much as we love ourselves. One way we can get to know and love God better is to read his words to us in his book 'the Bible'. So today we will be getting to grips with the Bible and grappling with such questions as (shouted out by Question Mark):

- *What's the Bible all about?*
- *Who wrote it and where did it come from?*
- *Why should I read it?*
- *Where do I start?*
- *And what will it do for me?*

 The book of books

A quiz
6 mins

This activity introduces the contents of the Bible by comparing it to a selection of other books. Ask for between two and six volunteers to compete in the Book of Books quiz show. Sit them in two teams each with some kind of buzzer, whistle or bell. Explain that you are going to show them a range of books from personal diaries through to the Guinness Book of Records. They have to identify what the book has in common with the Bible. If they wish to answer they should ring their bell or blow their whistle. If their answer is correct they score a point, but if not the question is passed over to the other team. When you display each book make it clear what kind of book it is. If, for example, you are displaying the novel *Treasure Island* introduce it as 'a novel', otherwise they might get distracted by the fact it is one particular novel. Here is a list of suggested books for you to display. You don't have to use them all, but you should be able to get hold of most without too much trouble.

BOOK	SIMILARITIES WITH BIBLE
Any guide book	*guide to life*
Any instruction manual	*practical instructions about living*
Any good novel	*full of excellent stories*
Complete works of Shakespeare	*classic literature about human lives*
Any book of poems	*contains poetry*
Any book of proverbs	*contains wise advice*
Any book of morals or religious teaching	*contains moral teaching*
Any history book	*contains history*
A diary	*contains people's personal thoughts*
Any text book	*worth studying*
Romantic novel or book on relationships	*contains plenty of romance and advice*
Biography	*contains biographies of people who knew God*

Any theology or philosophy book	*contains wisdom on the meaning of life*
Any book of questions and answers	*answers life questions*
Guinness Book of Records	*contains some of the most extraordinary facts in human history*

This'll be that letter from God I've been waiting for!

A Bible advert

Run a book review of the Bible as a way of summing up the Book of Books Quiz. Read the following script in a deep, smooth voice over the backing track on the audio cassette.

There now follows an advertisement for the Bible:

The Bible is God's own book. Its central characters are God, his Son Jesus and his Holy Spirit. The plot unfolds God's rescue plan for the human race and reaches its terrifying climax in the brutal execution of his Son Jesus.

Over the centuries millions upon millions of people have heard God speaking to them through the words of the Bible. This is because God brings the Bible alive and through it can lead you into a vital relationship with him.

The Bible is a down-to-earth and practical book. It doesn't flinch from the tough issues and deals fairly and squarely with such questions as 'Who is God?' 'Why does God allow suffering?' and 'Why are we alive?' All that we have said in Getting to Grips with God *has been based on the words of the Bible.*

So, if you want to get to know God, read his own book. If you want guidelines on how to live your life, read the maker's instruction manual. If you want your life questions answered then read God's answer book. If you just want a ripping good read, pick up the Holy Bible. It is available at a good bookshop near you. You won't be the same again.

Can I believe it?

Conduct a TV chat show type interview with a Bible expert about the reliability of the Bible. Below are a few questions and answers that you could work round.

- **What evidence is there for the Christian belief that the Bible is God's book?**

   Some of the most convincing evidence for the claim that the Bible is nothing other than God's handiwork is its astonishing unity of message. Now I would just like to carry out an experiment here. *(Hand out slips of paper and pens and get everyone to write down a description of what has happened in the meeting so far. Collect them in and read some of them out. Pick up on any contradictions and make the point that the accounts vary considerably despite the fact you have all been in the same meeting.)* Go on to make the point that the Bible, in contrast, has an extraordinary unity. This is remarkable considering that it was written over a period of about 1,500 years by more than forty different authors of very varied backgrounds, cultures and education. Joshua, for example, was a military general, Daniel was a prime minister, Peter was a fisherman and Nehemiah was a royal cup-bearer. A mixed bunch. What is more, it was written in three different continents, Africa, Asia, Europe, and in three different languages Hebrew, Aramaic, Greek. Despite this there is an astonishing agreement in its message. If we couldn't even come up with a unified account of what has happened in this meeting, it is absolutely astonishing that a book written over such a huge time scale, by such a range of authors could have such a unified account of God's plan for human history. That is one reason why we can be confident that God is behind it.

- **What evidence is there for believing that the Bible is historically reliable?**

Well, let's think about the record of the life of Jesus. The people who wrote biographies of Jesus either knew the man personally or knew someone who did. It is therefore reasonable to assume that their facts were accurate.

- **But perhaps they just got carried away and started exaggerating and making wild claims for Jesus?**

When their accounts of the life of Jesus were written there would have been many people who knew Jesus who were still alive. If Mark and John had been telling lies I think they would have faced considerable opposition.

- **But perhaps their accounts of Jesus' life have been changed over the years?**

There are a considerable number of very early New Testament manuscripts around today. Over 5,500 copies contain all or part of the New Testament. There are two *complete* copies dating from 250 years from the time of writing, and there are many earlier fragments some dating from only 30 years from moment when the authors put pen to paper. This may sound like a long time, but by ancient history standards this is peanuts. The earliest copy of Caesar's *Gallic Wars* for example dates from 1,000 years after it was written. Sir Frederic Kenyon, world expert on ancient manuscripts and former director of the British Museum, said that, *'The interval between the dates of original composition (of the New Testament) and the earliest (surviving) evidence becomes so small as to be in fact negligible, and the last foundations for any doubt that the Scriptures have come down to us substantially as they were written has now been removed.'*[4]

- **What other evidence do you have that the Bible is God's book?**

Well, there is considerable evidence and arguments for this belief, but I would like to say that at the end of the day the proof of the pudding is in the eating. We need to read the Bible ourselves if we are to make up our mind about whether it is God's book to us or not. I have found that God has spoken to me through it and I'm convinced, but we all need to read it ourselves before deciding one way or the other.

The Hot Seat

Interrogation time
4 mins

Set up the Hot Seat and light and play the Hot Seat theme tune. Let the group interrogate a leader or guest about their relationship with the Bible. Do remember that a desire to get stuck into Bible reading is caught not taught—if you are obviously hooked on the Bible, your enthusiasm will be contagious. Here are a couple of questions you could use to set the ball rolling:

- *What is special to you about the Bible?*
- *What would you say to someone who thought the Bible was dead boring?*

Smash 'n' Grab

Getting the point
2 mins

Set up the Smash 'n' Grab screen and let them do their weekly chat. Remember what you see on the screen is what the group will see, so make it dramatic!

Grab: Hi, Smash! *(wave)*
Smash: Hi-ya, Grab! *(take five or shake hands)* 'Ow ya doin', mate?

Grab:	No too bad, thanks. *(thumbs up)*
Smash:	'Ave ya got the point, then?
Grab:	The point of what? *(palm up)*
Smash:	The point of the meetin'.
Grab:	Na, can't see it, mate. *(palm down)*
Smash:	*(pointing)* Well, the point is that God has given us his special book, the Bible, so that we can get to know him better.
Grab:	Oh right! Gotcha. The Bible tells us what God is really like. If we get to grips with that we'll get to grips with him. Now that you've pointed it out I see it. *(Smash paper and grab point.)* I've got the point!
Smash:	You've got it, mate. You've got the point! *(thumbs up)*

Any answers

Qs & As
2 mins

Answer any questions in the box from last week. Don't forget that there are some sample answers to common questions at the end of this book. See page 119.

Activities

First impressions

Bible thoughts
2 mins

Welcome everyone to your small activity group and give them a chance to chat together. Then hand out copies of the worksheets and ask them to jot down the first thoughts that come into their heads when they think of the Bible. Encourage a few people to share their first impressions.

Bible pass the parcel

A game with a
message
8 mins

This game of pass the parcel with a difference aims to get across a lot of information about the Bible in an enjoyable way. Play the game exactly as you would play an ordinary game of pass the parcel. Pass a large multi-layered parcel round the group to music. When the music stops, the person holding the parcel has to unwrap one layer. Normally there would be little presents or sweets concealed between layers, but with Bible pass the parcel the layers contain interesting facts and puzzling objects about the Bible.

Here are some examples of objects and facts for you to put in the parcel. Try to alternate the objects and facts between layers.

Objects
Attach a label to each object saying, 'In what way is this object like the Bible?' Get the unwrapper to have a guess, then take other suggestions.

- A key (the Bible unlocks the meaning of life)
- A map (the Bible is our guide through life)

- A small sword (the Bible is a weapon that cuts through to the heart of the matter)
- A piece of bread (the Bible is food)
- An instruction manual (the Bible is like the Maker's instruction manual)
- A telephone (you can hear God speak to you in the words of the Bible)
- A squashed milk carton (the Bible is essential to our growth and development just as milk is essential to a new-born baby)

Interesting facts

Ask the unwrapper to read out their fact about the Bible.

- The word Bible comes from the Greek word *biblia* which means 'books'. The Bible is not just one book, it is in fact sixty-six books—a whole library.
- The Bible is split into two parts. The first is called the Old Testament and consists of thirty-nine books. It tells the story of God's dealing with the Hebrew nation before Jesus came.
- The second part of the Bible is called the New Testament and has twenty-seven books. This tells of the birth, life, death and resurrection of Jesus. It also describes the growth of Christianity and gives practical advice on how to live as a follower of Jesus.
- The Bible took about 1,500 years to be completed. It was written by about forty people among whom were a king, a doctor, a taxman and a fisherman.
- The central plot of the Bible is about God's rescue plan for the human race.
- St Paul wrote the following words about the Bible (Scripture) to his friend Timothy: 'All Scripture is inspired by God and is useful for teaching the truth, rebuking error, correcting faults, and giving instruction for right living, so that the person who serves God may be fully qualified and equipped to do every kind of good deed.'

When you have finished and cleared up the mess ask everyone to jot down in the worksheets all they can remember about the Bible from the pass the parcel game. Discuss what you've written and check that you've got all the points.

Can I recommend some light reading, madam?

Role plays
10 mins

Split into pairs and ask each pair to devise a role play where one of them is a bookshop sales assistant trying to sell a Bible to an interested customer. The idea is that the sales assistant explains what the Bible is all about and why it is such an important book. Either get back together and perform them to each other or swap roles after five minutes and try it again.

Practical Bible reading hints

Top tips
4 mins

Give the group a short introduction to finding your way round the Bible. Here is a rough outline:

1. Explain that the Bible is not a novel but a set of books. It is not sensible to start at page one and read all the way through. It is more like a library and you need to choose a book that is suitable for you. Mark's Gospel is ideal for new Christians.

2. Many people find using daily Bible reading notes helps them understand the Bible and apply it to their lives. Perhaps you could run a book review for the *Getting to Grips with God* daily readings.

3. Explain how to find your way round the Bible. The Bible is divided into books, chapters and verses. For example:

- 'John' is the name of the book (use the index to find out what page it starts on)
- 'chapter 3' is the chapter
- 'verse 16' is the verse (each chapter is split into numbered sentences or verses)
- show how the verse is written: e.g. John 3:16 or John 3 verse 16

Hands-on experience

A Bible reading workshop
8 mins

An ideal way to give them a taste of Bible reading is to work through a *Getting to Grips with God* sample reading together. One of these is included in the worksheet. Work through it together and as you do it together make the following points:

- *Try and find a quiet place and a regular time (5 mins).*
- *Ask God to help you understand what you read.*
- *Read the Bible passage and the comment on it.*
- *Do the activity or answer the questions. These will help you understand what the passage is all about.*
- *Ponder or pray about what passage has to say.*

Pray this

Praying together
4 mins

Developing the theme of the sample daily Bible reading, encourage the group to write prayers to God about his instruction manual in the space provided on the worksheet. Perhaps they could ask him to help them learn to use it or thank him for it. Then pass the wrapped present (or other object) round the group so that everyone knows when to pray their prayer, whether silently or out loud.

Taking stock

The crunch
2 mins

Ask the group to complete the 'Taking stock' questions on the worksheets. If there is time perhaps you could all share what you have learnt.

- *How has your attitude to the Bible changed in this meeting?*
- *How might this affect your life?*

Getting to Grips with
the Holy Spirit

The Aim: To understand that the Holy Spirit is the Spirit of God who helps us become like Jesus.

The Lightning Bolt: John 14:16–17, 26.
Jesus on the Holy Spirit.

Equipment Checklist
PRESENTATIONS
❏ theme music
❏ Question Mark outfit
❏ wooden spoon & applause card
❏ Big Ben news chimes on tape
❏ water, ice, steam, egg & three glasses
❏ Hot Seat, light & theme music
❏ Smash 'n' Grab kit
❏ questions box

ACTIVITIES
❏ sticky labels
❏ worksheets & pens
❏ sheets of paper
❏ battery, egg, water, etc.
❏ magazines, scissors, glue

Letter to leaders

It is not easy to get a grip on the who, why and how of the Holy Spirit. In a nutshell the Holy Spirit is the Spirit of Jesus at work in human lives, doing today the very things that Jesus did for people two thousand years ago. The Holy Spirit lives in every Christian working to make them more like Jesus. He is a very busy person and we would save him a lot of time if we were more willing to cooperate.

Cooperation is needed in all working relationships. Friends who don't cooperate won't be friends for long. Business partners who refuse to cooperate won't be in business for long. A patient who won't cooperate with his dentist can't be treated. The patient might be in the dentist's surgery, but if he won't open his mouth the dentist can't sort out the painful tooth. In just the same way we have to cooperate with the Holy Spirit. The Spirit can only sort out the pain in our lives if we, like the dental patient, open up. The challenge for us is to cooperate with him just that little bit more than we did the day before. As cooperation grows, so does trust, and as trust grows the more the Holy Spirit is able to help us become like Jesus.

● **When did you last ask the Holy Spirit to fill you and to make you more like Jesus?**

● **How much do you trust God's Holy Spirit?**

Presentations

The whole presentations section of this meeting has been worked round the idea of a TV programme broadcast live from your youth group. For this you need a host, equipped with wooden spoon microphone, to link the different sections of the programme. Perhaps you could have a large 'APPLAUSE' card that you could hold up at the appropriate moments.

 ## Leading questions

Welcome & introduction
2 mins

The host kicks off the programme something like this: *Hello and welcome to a live edition of* Getting to Grips with God. *Today we are the guests of St Ethelred's youth group in Basingstoke* (name of your group). *St Ethelreds was built in...* (date) *in the...* (name of district) *area of the city. It has a lively membership of...* (number of members) *and among its claims to fame is...* (some interesting fact).

In the last two editions of Getting to Grips with God *we have been investigating how Christians can love God more fully. We have investigated the role of prayer and the Bible in this process and today we will be looking at that vital power source behind Christian living, the Holy Spirit, and grappling with such issues as* (shouted out by Question Mark):

- *Who is the Holy Spirit?*
- *How's he related to God?*
- *What's his line of business?*
- *How do I know if I've got him?*
- *What difference would it make if I had?*

 ## The background

Imagine this
4 mins

The host continues: *Ladies and gentlemen I would like you to cast your minds back nearly 2,000 years. Picture the scene. You are one of Jesus' disciples. You have followed him closely for three years, giving up everything to be with him. You believe that he is God's long awaited saviour of the human race. You are thrilled to be in his closest circle of followers and deeply excited to see how he is going to rescue planet earth from the grips of evil and sin.*

Lately you have noticed a certain grim determination in your friend and master and sense that something big is about to happen. He has brought you all to Jerusalem to celebrate the Passover. It is a Thursday night and you are gathered together to eat the Passover meal. You and the other disciples are in a state of high excitement, but Jesus, well you've never seen him like this. Something is weighing heavily on his mind and you can't puzzle it out.

Then he drops the bombshell. He quietens you down and slowly explains that tomorrow he is going to give up his life. He will be handed over to be executed by crucifixion. It is God's master plan (you don't understand that bit). He says that there is no turning back, for this is what he came for.

Slowly the reality dawns. He is leaving you. He is not going to be around any more. You don't understand what he's up to, but you know that this is the end. Desperate headlines flash across the TV screen of your mind: (play the Big Ben news chimes on the audio cassette and get someone else to read the following headlines between each chime).

- DISCIPLES STRANDED HELPLESS
- BEST FRIEND WALKS OUT—FOLLOWERS FACE LIFE ALONE
- GOD NOW UNKNOWABLE—HEAVENLY HOT LINE AXED
- LIFE EMPTY AS GOD–MAN EXITS
- LECTURES OVER: NO MORE LESSONS FOR LIFE
- MIRACLE MEMORIES BOUND TO FADE

Jesus on the Holy Spirit

Bible reading
2 mins

Well, ladies and gentlemen, Jesus could see these panic headlines in his disciples' eyes. So he went on to explain the next part of God's master plan. A stroke of genius designed especially to meet the needs of his followers after he had gone. This is what he told them:

Jesus said to his disciples, 'I will ask the Father, and he will give you another Helper, who will stay with you for ever. He is the Spirit who reveals the truth about God. The world cannot receive him, because it cannot see him or know him. But you know him, because he remains with you and is in you… The Helper, the Holy Spirit, whom the Father will send in my name, will teach you everything and make you remember all that I have told you' (John 14:16–17, 26).

This was good news for the disciples. Their panic headlines were replaced one by one by astonishing new ones describing what the Holy Spirit would do for them. (Read these out with more Big Ben chimes.)

- HOLY SPIRIT HELP AT HAND
- FOLLOWERS FIND FOREVER FRIEND
- GOD'S TRUTHS PERSONALLY REVEALED
- GOD MOVES INTO HUMAN LIVES
- HEAVENLY PERSONAL TUTOR STARTS WORK
- MIRACLE MEMORIES NOW MEMORIZED

Who is the Holy Spirit?

A tough
question
3 mins

Ladies and gentlemen, we've looked at the background to the sending of the Holy Spirit and now we are going to tackle some tough questions about him. Over to Jane (person answering questions).

Perhaps 'Jane' could plant the question 'Who is the Holy Spirit?' in the questions box and answer it something like this:

So who is the Holy Spirit? Well, this is a very good question and the answer is not too easy to grasp. God is really three different and distinct persons—God the Father, God the Son (Jesus) and God the Holy Spirit. Though they are three distinct persons they are at the same time one God. How can that be so? The illustration of water may help…

Water, ice and steam

Take a glass of water, some ice and a boiling kettle and explain that water comes in three states. Plain old water becomes solid (ice) when the temperature drops below 0 ℃. When it is heated to 100 ℃ it boils and becomes steam. Steam and ice are still water, but are in different states at different temperatures. It is rather like that with God. If you imagine that God the Father is like the water, then Jesus is God made solid like the ice, and the Holy Spirit is God spreading everywhere like the steam.

Egg

Another good illustration is that of the egg. Take an egg, crack it and separate the yolk, white and shell into three glasses. Explain that the one egg consists of three parts: shell, white and yoke. The three parts make up one egg. In the same way, though there is only one God there are three distinct parts to him.

Conclude by saying that the answer to the question 'Who is the Holy Spirit?' is that he is the Spirit of God, and is as much God as God the Father and God the Son.

What does the Holy Spirit do?

A tough question

3 mins

Plant the question 'What does the Holy Spirit do?' in the box and answer it like this:

As we saw in meeting three, Jesus was none other than the invisible God made visible—God living a human life. 2,000 years ago he walked the face of planet earth helping the people he met to get to know God and live in the way that he wanted them to. Unfortunately, Jesus couldn't be everywhere at once and couldn't stay around for ever, so the help he could give to human beings was limited to the few who were around with him. That doesn't include you or me or 99.99 per cent of the world's population. To solve this problem Jesus promised that when he had gone he would send the Holy Spirit to be with and help the remaining 99.99 per cent of the world's population who wanted to follow him. God gives us the Holy Spirit when we ask Jesus to be 'in charge' of our lives and his job is to give us the power to follow Jesus and become more like him.

To demonstrate this get hold of a couple of battery-powered radios and remove the batteries before the meeting. Ask for two volunteers and explain that you want them to tune in to a chosen radio station as quickly as possible. Put the radios a couple of meters away from the contestants and start the race with a ready, steady, go. It shouldn't be long before they realize that they have been set up and that the batteries are missing. The obvious point is that without power the radios can't fulfil the task for which they were designed. Explain that it is just like that with you and me. We were designed to be like Jesus (made in God's image), but without the help of the Holy Spirit we are powerless and can't fulfil our potential.

Wey hey! I surrender

THAT'S MY BOY

HOLY SPIRIT

The Hot Seat

Interrogation time
4 mins

Set up the Hot Seat and light and play the Hot Seat theme music. Introduce this week's guest to the audience and explain that members of the studio audience are now going to ask the guest questions about their experience of the Holy Spirit. If necessary set the ball rolling by asking a couple of questions of your own. Here are a couple you could use:

- *How do you know that the Holy Spirit is at work in you?*
- *What difference does the Holy Spirit make to your life?*

Any answers

Qs & As
4 mins

Answer any questions put in the box at the last meeting. Try and keep your answers short, clear and to the point. Conclude this live edition of *Getting to Grips with God* by summing up what you have discovered about the Holy Spirit and handing over to Smash 'n' Grab.

Smash 'n' Grab

Getting the point
2 mins

Set up the Smash 'n' Grab screen and introduce Smash and Grab. Run the concluding conversation along the following lines.

Grab:	Hi, Smash! *(wave)*
Smash:	Hi-ya, Grab! *(shake hands)* 'Ow ya doin', mate?
Grab:	No too bad, thanks. *(thumbs up)*
Smash:	'Ave ya got the point, then?
Grab:	The point of what? *(palm up)*
Smash:	The point of the meetin'.
Grab:	Na, can't see it, mate. *(palm down)*
Smash:	*(pointing)* Well, the point is that God sent the Holy Spirit to help us become like Jesus.
Grab:	Right! So the Holy Spirit gives us the kind of help Jesus gave his disciples 2,000 years ago. Now that you've pointed it out, I can see it. *(smash paper and grab point.)* I've got the point!
Smash:	You've got it, mate. You've got the point! *(thumbs up)*

Activities

Imitators

A guessing game
12 mins

The aim of this game is to help the group understand what it means to become like Jesus and that it is impossible to do so without the Holy Spirit's help. Write out the names of various famous or fictitious characters on separate sticky labels. Sit everyone in a circle facing inwards and stick a label on each person's forehead. Explain that they have to work out whose name is written on their forehead by taking it in turn to ask questions that have the answer 'Yes' or 'No' (e.g. Am I alive? Am I on TV?). Work round the group a few times letting each person ask a question. Then give clues to anyone who still hasn't guessed. Once everyone has worked out who they are ask them the following questions.

- *How much do you want to be like that person?*
- *How hard would it be to imitate them?*

Then ask them similar questions about Jesus (on worksheets) and conclude by explaining that the job of the Holy Spirit is to help us all to become like Jesus.

- *How much would you like to be like Jesus?*
- *How hard would you find it to imitate him?*
- *Where would you get it wrong most often?*

Jobs of the Holy Spirit

A self-inflicted quiz
15 mins

Hand out the worksheets and read John 14:16–17, 26 together. Split into two teams and explain that each team has five minutes both to familiarize themselves with the passage and write ten tricky questions on it for the other group to answer. These questions should be written on a separate piece of paper from the worksheets. Then get back together, make sure all the worksheets are out of sight and let the two teams put their questions to each other in turn. The teams score a point if they can correctly answer the opposition's question. You will need to judge if the questions are fair. Here are two examples, the first of which is fair and the second not.

- *Which comes first in the passage? The point that the Holy Spirit will stay with us for ever, or the point that the Holy Spirit is in us?*
- *How many times does the word 'you' feature in the passage?*

Holy Spirit fact file

Summing up
5 mins

To recap on what you have learnt ask the group to jot down in their worksheets all that they know about the Holy Spirit under the heading 'Holy Spirit fact file' and 'Object lessons' This involves listing the six jobs of the Holy Spirit mentioned in the passage highlighted in **bold**, jotting down the point of the three Holy Spirit illustrations and anything else they know about the Holy Spirit. Go round the group with each person sharing one thing until you run out.

Go on to ask if someone would like to explain what an egg tells us about the Holy Spirit. Give them an egg and three glasses and let them have a go. Then produce a battery and ask if someone would like to explain its link with the Holy Spirit and do the same with the water. This will enable you to find out how much they understand about the Holy Spirit and discuss any outstanding questions.

Becoming like Jesus

Collages
15 mins

This activity aims to help the group compare what they are like now with the way God would like them to be. Get hold of a selection of magazines and newspapers, scissors and glue. Hand everyone two bits of A4 paper and ask them to make two collages, one describing what they are like now (words and images about their personalities, the things they are good and bad at, etc.) and the other describing the way Jesus wants them to be. If you don't have time to make collages, simply write words into the frames on the worksheets. Once they have finished, explain that the job of the Holy Spirit is to make them like Jesus and like their second collage. St Paul puts it like this: *'Those whom God had already chosen he also set apart to become like his Son'* (Romans 8:29).

Taking stock

The crunch
4 mins

Ask the group to complete the questions under the 'Taking stock' heading in their worksheets. If appropriate go on to discuss their answers.

- *Do you want to become more like Jesus?*
- *Are you ready to let the Holy Spirit start working on you?*

Prayer letters

Dear God . . .
5 mins

Encourage each person to write a letter to God about the changes that they would like him to help them make in their lives in the space provided on the worksheets. Once they have had time to do this have a time of quiet when they can read their letter to God silently and ask him to help them.

Getting to Grips with
God's Family

The Aim: To discover that every Christian is a member of God's family and that we should care for each other.

The Lightning Bolt: Acts 2:42–47.
Life among the first believers.

Equipment Checklist:

PRESENTATIONS
- ❏ theme music
- ❏ Question Mark outfit
- ❏ worksheets & pens
- ❏ family photo album
- ❏ HWG acetates and theme music
- ❏ food processor
- ❏ Hot Seat, light & theme music
- ❏ Smash 'n' Grab kit
- ❏ questions box

ACTIVITIES
- ❏ worksheets & pens
- ❏ limerick slips
- ❏ ball of string

Letter to leaders

Having lived in Bristol my entire life I have just moved to Exeter with Jane and her job. This was potentially quite a lonely experience as I knew no one in Exeter and would not meet people through my job (as I work at home alone). We immediately made contact with the local church and came to realize in a new way what a family the church is. People whom we have never met before have shown us love and kindness and made us feel welcome. 'Lost relatives return to Exeter!' We have been made aware that we are part of an enormous family bound together by a common experience of God's love and forgiveness.

It is so easy to forget that many many people don't have the security of being part of this unique family. They may well get by on their own, but having relatives round every corner (of the globe) does make moving cities easier. Membership of God's family, however, should not just be about having our needs met. God wants us in turn to pass the love that we receive on to those outside his family and beyond. God gives us his love and expects to see it recycled and redistributed.

- *Imagine how your life would be different if you weren't a member of God's family.*

- *What can you do to make others feel more welcome in God's family in your area?*

Presentations

 **Leading questions**

Welcome & introduction
1 min

Have the theme music playing as the group arrives and give them a warm welcome. Remind the group how in the last three *Getting to Grips with God* meetings you have been exploring how prayer, the Bible and the Holy Spirit help us love God with all our hearts. Go on to explain that our love for God should affect all our relationships and today you will be getting to grips with being part of God's family and grappling with such questions as (shouted out by Question Mark):

- *Why does God have a family?*
- *Who is in his family?*
- *What happens at family parties?*
- *Does God's family need me?*
- *How can I be a good family member?*

 Meet the family

Getting to know you
7 mins

This is a game to get everyone mixing with the other members of God's family in your group. Hand out the worksheets and pens and give everyone five minutes to go round the group and collect the signatures of people who fit the ten descriptions. Once time is up find out who falls into each of the categories.

- *Who has more than two brothers or sisters?*
- *Who is a vegetarian?*
- *Who is the oldest child in their family?*
- *Who has a mum who is under 34 years old?*
- *Who became a Christian this year?*
- *Who says they never argue with their parents?*
- *Who has a grandparent living in their house?*
- *Who has a baby brother or sister (under 2)?*
- *Who has a relation who is a twin?*
- *Who has more than ten letters in their surname?*

 Happy families

Photo albums
2 mins

Explain to the group that when we ask Jesus to be 'in charge' of our lives we become God's children and join his family. God is our father and other believers are our brothers and sisters! This meeting is really a family get-together; God's family meeting together. Get everyone to look around the room and tell them that they are all related to each other. Show the group one of your family photo albums and draw out some of the things that your family does together: picnics, sharing major life experiences such as weddings, funerals, births, growing up together. Members of God's family should share their lives with each other in just the same way.

Family policy

*Hindley Watson
Grouch MP
4 mins*

This is a story about The Rt Hon. Richard Hindley Watson Grouch MP and his attempt to turn his idea of society as a big family into policy. The real aim of the story is to explore the way in which the first Christians behaved like one big family, as recorded in Acts 2:42–47. Ideally you need two people to read alternate paragraphs of the story. Play the Hindley Watson Grouch theme tune (on the audio cassette) in the background as you read and display the six illustrations on pages 98–103 on an OHP.

(PICTURE 1) The Rt Hon. Richard Hindley Watson Grouch MP was a man of great and noble character who worked tirelessly for the good of this great and noble country of ours. His impressive career in parliament had taken him through the following notable posts.

Coordinator of the Houses of Parliament tea rota.

Under Secretary to the Junior Minister for the Abolition of the Homeless.

But now, at the tender age of fifty-six, he had risen to the giddy heights of Secretary of State for the Creation of a Caring Country.

The first thing the Rt Hon. Richard Hindley Watson Grouch MP did in his new post was familiarize himself with his brief, which ran something like this:

Sort out problem of social inequality.

Reverse trend of increasing drug abuse, homelessness, crime and suicide in young people.

Make country seem a more caring place.

(PICTURE 2) While he pondered these great problems, he had a flash of inspiration. Society, he thought, should be like 'one big family'. We should all love and care for each other. Yes, 'the family' was the perfect analogy. He would phone the PM straight away… On second thoughts perhaps he ought to do a bit of research first.

He arranged a meeting with his research team and explained his remarkable idea. 'Was there', he asked, 'any precedent for suggesting that the ideal society should be like a caring family?' His researchers raised an eyebrow and promised to find out.

(PICTURE 3) A week later they reported back. To Hindley Watson Grouch's slight annoyance his brainwave was not totally original. According to his research team this concept was fully developed and lived out by the followers of a religious leader in Palestine nearly 2,000 years ago and is still practised by them today.

'What's the man's name?' asked Hindley Watson Grouch.

'Jesus of Nazareth,' came the reply. Hindley Watson Grouch thought he had heard of him. 'Well, tell me about this man and what his followers did.'

'Well, sir, according to a very early document called "The Acts of the Apostles" these first "Christians", as they were known, numbered over 5,000 and behaved like a remarkably close family.'

'Go on,' said Hindley Watson Grouch.

'Well, sir they had their meals together in their homes.'

(PICTURE 4) 'Good idea,' said Hindley Watson Grouch. 'We'll make people do the same. I can see it now, "The Bill for the Introduction of Compulsory Meals with Neighbours". Splendid. Go on.'

(PICTURE 3) **'The document says that "They sold their property and possessions, and distributed the money among all, according to what each one needed. They also shared their belongings with one another." '**

'I see,' said Hindley Watson Grouch. 'That could prove tricky, but that's definitely the kind of spirit we need to create if we are going to make this country caring.'

'Er, I don't mean to be indelicate, sir, but would you be prepared to sell your three Rolls Royces and distribute the money between your more needy neighbours?'

The Rt Hon. Richard Hindley Watson Grouch MP looked mildly annoyed and replied that he couldn't see what that had to do with it.

(PICTURE 5) **'Well, sir, shall we go on? It appears that the leaders of these first Christians performed miracles and wonders that filled everyone with awe. I don't suppose that this would be essential in our situation, but if you could produce the odd miracle, sir, it would certainly help launch the campaign for the new Caring Community.'**

Hindley Watson Grouch wondered about this, but since he had never been credited with performing miracles in the past (apart from the time he offered to help with the washing up) he doubted that he would be able to manage it. Yet, undaunted, he pressed on with his policy plans for the new Caring Family Society.

(PICTURE 3) **'Well, sir,' his researcher continued, 'it appears that these first Christians met regularly in the Jerusalem temple and spent their time praising and praying to God. I think we need to face the fact that these "Christians" had some strange motivation in their caring for each other. It seems that God was something to do with it.'**

Hindley Watson Grouch looked puzzled. 'Correct me if I'm wrong,' he replied, 'but you're saying that God was inspiring them to invite each other round for meals and sell their possessions? You think that it would not have happened if he wasn't behind them?'

'I think you might be right, sir,' came the reply.

'I see,' said Hindley Watson Grouch. But he probably didn't because he then said, 'I dare say if we portray the Government as some kind of authoritative 'God' figure that knows what's best for the people, everyone will fall in behind and do what we tell them, what ho!'

'Well, sir,' his advisers replied, 'we can't be sure of that... But we do have one very encouraging piece of information about these first Christians. They were incredibly popular. The document says that "they enjoyed the good will of all the people and that every day the Lord added to their group those who were being saved." '

(PICTURE 6) Hindley Watson Grouch's eyes lit up. 'What splendid news!' he boomed. 'This is just the kind of boost the party needs in the run-up to the next election. Once we get the message out about our new "Caring Community", our "Family of Friends", our "Sharing Society", people will come flocking to join the party. I must say I'm a genius.'

Well, I'm sorry to say that there was one fatal flaw in the Rt Hon. Richard Hindley Watson Grouch MP's marvellous theory. I'm sure you can see what it is.

Just remember not to make the same mistake yourself.

The Right Honourable
Mr Richard Hindley Watson Grench M.P.

1

Flash of Inspiration!

3

Miracle Man!

6

The parable of the food processor

An illustration
2 mins

Get hold of a food processor and talk the group through what food processors tell us about the family of God. Here is a rough outline:

The family of God is like a food processor. This may surprise you but, just like the family of God, the food processor is made up of lots of individual bits: motor, plug, container and lid. The job of the food processor is to process food. But each bit on its own is completely useless. What use is a lid on its own? It's useless. What use is a container with a blade in? Useless. What use is a motor? Useless. What use is a plug? Useless.

In the same way you and I, the individual members of the family of God, are pretty useless on our own and not able to fulfil our potential. But when you put all the bits together (assemble food processor) and plug it in… hey presto! It's incredibly useful. It processes food! Like the individual parts of the food processor, we Christians are designed to work in a team. When all the members of God's family are working together, supporting each other and plugged into God, things really start happening.

The Hot Seat

Interrogation time
4 mins

Set up the Hot Seat and light and play the Hot Seat theme music. Let the group grill the inhabitant of this week's chair about their experience of being a member of God's family. You might need to set the ball rolling with some questions of your own. Here are a couple you could to use:

- *What is the best and worst thing about being in God's family?*
- *Have you ever been really helped in a crisis by another Christian?*

Smash 'n' Grab

Getting the point
2 mins

Set up the back-lit Smash 'n' Grab screen and let them have the following conversation:

Grab: Hi, Smash! *(wave)*

Smash: Hi-ya, Grab! *(take five or shake hands)* 'Ow ya doin', mate?

Grab: Fine, thanks. *(thumbs up)*

Smash: 'Ave ya got the point, then?

Grab: The point of what? *(palm up)*

Smash: The point of the meetin'.

Grab: Na, can't see it, mate. *(palm down)*

Smash: *(pointing)* Well, the point is that we're all members of God's family and we have a responsibility to care for each other.

Grab: Oh right! Gotcha. I'm part of a huge worldwide family, and God wants me to look after all my brothers and sisters. Now that you've pointed it out, I can see it. *(Smash paper and grab point.)* I've got the point!

Smash: You've got it, mate. You've got the point! *(thumbs up)*

Any answers

Answer any questions put in the box at the last meeting. Remind everyone about the box and encourage them to keep posting their queries.

What? Am I related to all of them?!

Activities

Building families

A game
5 mins

This is a game to get everyone working together as a team. Explain that you want them to use their bodies to spell out the word TEAM. (A person standing with their arms held wide apart will make a 'T' shape. The 'E' can be made by a person standing sideways with both hands held in front of them and a second person sitting on the first person's feet, legs and hands out horizontally in front.) Once they have made the word TEAM, get them to try and make the word FAMILY and then LOVE. If you are doing this with a large group split them into teams of about eight and do it as a race.

Family acts

Split the group into two teams. Explain that there is a passage in the Bible describing ten ways in which the first Christians treated each other like one big family. You want a volunteer from each team to collect from you one of these 'family actions' and then go and mime it out for the other members of the team to guess. Once they have guessed it another member of the team should come and tell you what the mime was and collect the next one to mime to the group. Carry on like this until one team has mimed and guessed all ten.

- *They learnt from the disciples.*
- *They praised God in the temple.*
- *They were close friends.*
- *They had meals together.*
- *They prayed together.*
- *They sold their property and shared out the money.*
- *They shared their belongings.*
- *The disciples performed miracles.*
- *They were very popular.*
- *They invited new people to join the family.*

Love in action

Read together the account of the first Christians' family behaviour on the worksheets. Then get each person to list the ten things these first Christians did under the 'Family act List' heading. Go on to explain that their behaviour is a role model to inspire us and that you want them to compose a limerick about a person who followed their example. Write out the following limerick first lines on separate pieces of paper, hand them out and ask the group to complete them. Perhaps you could read the completed limerick starting *'Each Friday when Jill got her pay'* to give them the idea. (A limerick is a five line comic poem in which the first, second and fifth lines rhyme, as do the third and fourth: you know the sort of thing.) Get back together and read them to each other.

- *Each Friday when Jill got her pay . . .*
- *When Horace saw Bill all alone . . .*
- *When Mary had smashed up her car . . .*
- *When Sidney was not very well . . .*
- *While Peter was baking a cake . . .*
- *Having gone to the chapel to pray . . .*
- *Charlene, worried sick for her friend . . .*
- *A keen new recruit known as Kate . . .*
- *When the vicar was feeling depressed . . .*
- *Matilda was full of God's love . . .*

Each Friday when Jill got her pay
She'd treat herself daft—come what may,
But since she's met God
She thinks this is odd
And instead gives the whole lot away.

Bound together

All tied together
3 mins

Remind the group that once we ask Jesus to be 'in charge' of our life, we join God's family and become brothers and sisters to each other. Sit everyone in a circle and take a large ball of string or wool. Hold on to one end and throw the ball to another member of the group, saying their name and adding the word 'brother' or 'sister' before it. They then hang on to the string and throw the ball to someone else and so on. Keep doing this until the whole group is bound together by a web of string. (Make sure that the string is thrown at least once to each group member.) While you all hold on to your bits of string explain that we are all bound together as members of God's family. We are there to support each other so that if one feels down in the dumps the others hold him or her up. The family of God gives us the strength and support to live for Jesus. Keep holding on to the string and go on to pray together…

Prayer support

Praying together
3 mins

If you feel that the group is happy and relaxed ask each person if there is one thing they would like prayed for. If you mention your prayer request first it will help them open up. It might also help if you mentioned the kind of things they might want prayed for, for example: grandparents, parents, brothers and sisters, pets, school, events in the news, etc. Once each person has had the opportunity to say something, perhaps they could each then pray a very simple prayer for the person on their left. If the person on their left hasn't mentioned anything they want prayed for suggest that they just say something like, 'Dear God, we pray you'll look after Pete. Amen'. Once you have all finished you can let go of the string.

Taking stock

The crunch
2 mins

Ask the group to fill in the 'Process this' and 'Taking stock' sections of the worksheet. If appropriate ask them to share what they have written.

- *What does the food processor tell you about being part of God's family?*
- *What have you discovered about being a member of God's family today?*
- *What one thing could you do this week to support your brothers and sisters in God's family?*

Getting to Grips with
Loving Others

 10

 The Aim: To understand that God wants us to love others as much we love ourselves.

 The Lightning Bolt: I Corinthians 13:4–7.
St Paul on love.

 Equipment Checklist

PRESENTATIONS
- ❏ theme music
- ❏ Question Mark outfit
- ❏ top ten backing track
- ❏ cured by love costumes
- ❏ Hot Seat, light & theme tune
- ❏ Smash 'n' Grab kit
- ❏ questions box

ACTIVITIES
- ❏ love songs on tape
- ❏ worksheets & pens
- ❏ copies of daily readings

Letter to leaders

 Mother Teresa once said, 'Now that you know how much God is in love with you, it is but natural that you spend the rest of your life radiating that love.'⁵ She certainly shows us how and we need to ask God to help us follow her example where we live and work.

For young people the challenge of showing love to others can be pretty daunting, or even out of the question. Simply surviving at school is bad enough, let alone trying to behave like Jesus. If you go out of your way to care for the unpopular members of the class you'll stand out like a sore thumb. It seems much safer to keep your head down.

Despite the difficulties, young people who have the support to really start living for Jesus at school can have a big impact. A friend told me about a thirteen year old girl in his youth group who was always bringing along new people to the group. He asked her what was the secret of her success, to which she replied, 'Well, I'm friendly with the people that no one else likes.' There was someone who understood the heart of Jesus! May there be many more like her.

- **How are you getting on learning to love your neighbour as you love yourself? Ask God to point you to someone whom he wants you to love in the coming week.**

- **Pray for each member of your group by name; that God would fill them with his Holy Spirit and give them a Jesus-like concern for others.**

Presentations

Leading questions

**Welcome &
introduction**
1 min

Have the theme music playing as the group arrives, and give them a warm welcome to the final *Getting to Grips with God* meeting. Remind them how over the last four meetings you have been investigating how we can love God with our whole heart. Go on to explain that our love for God should affect all our relationships: at school, with friends and at home. Jesus summed it up by saying, 'Love your neighbour as much as you love yourself'. In today's meeting you will be getting to grips with how you can do just that and grappling with questions such as (shouted by Question Mark):

- *What does God want me to do for him?*
- *What's love got to do with it?*
- *Why is it so powerful?*
- *How do I love my neighbour?*
- *And who is my neighbour anyway?*

Love's top ten

St Paul on love
2 mins

This is a presentation of St Paul's hymn to love in the style of a top ten hit parade. Play the backing track on the audio cassette and read it in your best 'top ten' voice.

OK, it's the moment we've all been waiting for. It's time for the Top Ten Love Hits of eternity compiled by that big-hearted man, Saint Paul of Tarsus.

10 *OK, yeah. Well, straight in at number ten is 'Love is patient and kind'—a quiet classic pulsating with serene energy.*

9 *Then at number nine we have the challenging operetta 'Love is not jealous or conceited or proud'.*

8 *In there at number eight is the gentleman's classic 'Love is not ill-mannered'.*

7 *At number seven is the hot, jazzy and disarmingly frank number 'Love's not selfish or irritable'. Despite a recent slating by the EGO magazine this is a real favourite.*

6 *Still in there at number six is the harmony on forgiveness 'Love does not keep a record of wrongs'.*

5 *Marching in at number five is the military sounding 'Love is not happy with evil'.*

4 *Standing firm at number four is the rich symphonic clarion call 'Love is happy with the truth'. Ever popular in an age of compromise.*

3 *Moving on to number three is the persistent solo piece 'Love never gives up'.*

2 *Still at number two the faultless theme and variation 'Love's faith, hope, and patience never fail'.*

1 *But at number one for the ninety-nine thousand, two hundred and sixty-eighth week is that endless hit anthem 'Love is eternal'. How much longer, we wonder, will it top the love hit parade? I have a feeling that it will be there for many aeons yet.*

Cured by love

Present this brief programme investigating 'love treatment', the new cure for a whole range of personal problems. There are three members of the cast: PROGRAMME PRESENTER, DR CARE ALOT and PATIENT MIKE. Here is a rough script for you to use.

PP Welcome to 'Medicine Matters'. In today's programme we are reporting on an astonishing new treatment for chronic disorders. We are here at the Cured by Love Centre in the village of Notsofar Fromyou in Wales. According to their own statistics the centre has a remarkable success rate at relieving a huge number of personal problems. These range from stress, depression, sleep disorders and general lack of well-being through to the more serious social problems of drug addiction, violent behaviour and criminality. The director of the centre is Dr Care Alot.

Dr Hello.

PP Dr Care Alot, could you tell us about the vision behind the Cured by Love Centre?

Dr The centre was set up five years here in Notsofar Fromyou, in the belief that love, L-O-V-E, can be an incredibly powerful force for good in human lives. When human beings are shown love, they respond in the most positive ways. We, here at the Cured by Love Centre, believe that many of the personal problems that people face may be caused by lack of love and are certainly curable by love treatment. Take the example of a young woman who has been receiving out-patient treatment at the centre. She came to us having attempted suicide. It later became apparent that throughout her childhood her parents showed her very little affection. She has now been through one of our programmes and is a changed woman.

PP So, what does the love treatment consist of, Dr Care Alot?

Dr Yes, that's a good question. It is really a very basic process. We simply show our visitors love. We care about them a lot. The staff here show respect for the individuals staying at the centre, they listen to them, and provide for all their needs in a warm and safe environment. Basically they become their friends. Of course, it is not simply a question of a week here and you're cured. It is an ongoing process. We enter into a contract of care with our friends. They know that we will go on loving them come what may.

PP Dr Care Alot, have you identified any absolutely essential ingredients in your treatments?

Dr It is absolutely essential that we really do care. It is no good pretending. That does not work. The staff here really do love and care for our visitors.

PP So, it appears that love is a very powerful force for good in the lives of human beings. Let's now meet some of the people who have received love treatment here at the centre. Mike Small, how has the centre helped you?

M Well, to be honest, I'd be sunk without this place. It's been a real godsend. To be honest, my life was a real mess; I had no friends, I couldn't sustain relationships, couldn't sleep at night, couldn't get a job. But anyway, I heard about this place and from the moment I walked in the door I felt different, like I really mattered and that these people cared.

PP So, what did they do for you?

M They just showed me love. It was that simple… And I'm hoping that they'll take me on as one of their volunteer staff. My life has been so changed by the Cured by Love Centre that I want to do something for other people who are in the mess I was.

PP Well, thank you, Mike. So, there you have it. Love treatment works. It may be that the power of love will be the medical discovery of the decade. The staff here at the Cured by Love Centre believe in it and the evidence is certainly convincing. The next step is a question of finding enough people who believe in the power of love and who are willing to offer the treatment to those who can benefit from it. That's all from Medicine Matters. Till next week, goodbye.

GOD'S GREAT RECYCLING PLAN

The power of love

Mother Teresa on love
1 min

Explain to the group who Mother Teresa is and perhaps tell them a little about her work with the destitute in Calcutta, then read the following extract from one of her books demonstrating the extraordinary power of love:

'Some months back a man who had been beaten up was picked up from the streets of Melbourne. He was an alcoholic who had been for years in that state, and the Sisters took him to their Home of Compassion. From the way they touched him, the way they took care of him, suddenly it was clear to him: "God loves me!" He left the home and never touched alcohol again, and went back to his family, to his children, to his job. Later, when he got his first salary, he came to the Sisters and gave them the money, saying: "I want you to be for others the love of God, as you have been to me." ' 6

The Hot Seat

Interrogation time
4 mins

Set up the Hot Seat and light and play the Hot Seat theme tune. Invite one of the leaders to take their place. Let the group grill them about their experiences of trying to show God's love to others. If necessary set the ball rolling with some questions of your own:

- *When was the last time you tried to show love to one of your 'neighbours'?*
- *Has someone showing you love ever made a difference to your life?*

Smash 'n' Grab

Getting the point
2 mins

Set up the Smash 'n' Grab screen and act out the following conversation:

Grab:	Hi, Smash! *(wave)*
Smash:	Hi-ya, Grab! *(take five or shake hands)* 'Ow ya doin', mate?
Grab:	Not too bad, thanks. *(thumbs up)*
Smash:	'Ave ya got the point, then?
Grab:	The point of what? *(palm up)*
Smash:	The point of the meetin'.
Grab:	Na, can't see it, mate. *(palm down)*
Smash:	*(pointing)* Well, the point is that God wants us to love other people as much as we love ourselves.
Grab:	Oh right! Gotcha. Now that we know that God loves us he wants us to love other people. Now that you've pointed it out, I can see it. *(Smash paper and grab point.)* I've got the point!
Smash:	You've got it, mate. You've got the point! *(thumbs up)*

Any answers

Qs & As
2 mins

Answer any questions in the box from last week. As it is the last meeting, perhaps you could suggest to the group that if anyone has any questions after *Getting to Grips with God* has finished they can always give you a ring.

Activities

Love songs

Sing along
5 mins

Collect a selection of love songs that are currently popular. Something that is being played a lot on a national popular radio station would do. You could borrow cassettes from the group members. Explain to the group that you are going to play a love song and you want the group to sing along (they will do this automatically if you pick popular songs). After about ten seconds turn the volume right down for five to ten seconds and then turn it back up. The idea is that the group keeps singing and is in time with the original when the volume is turned back up. This is easier said than done as the natural tendency is to sing faster. Once you've done a couple of songs together see if anyone wants to have a go on their own. Then discuss the messages of the different love songs. Remind the group that today you are looking at how God wants us to love others as much as we love ourselves. This is not a question of slushy romantic love (like the songs) but practical, down to earth caring.

The love test

How loving
are you?
10 mins

Hand out copies of the worksheet and ask the group to complete the St Paul's Love Test as honestly as possible. (See below for questions.) Then talk them through the scoring: *Score one point for each YES you have ticked for questions 1, 2, 8 & 9 and one point for each NO you have ticked for questions 3, 4, 5, 6, 7 & 10.* The nearer you are to ten then the more loving you are and vice versa. Don't force the group to reveal their scores!

1. *I am patient with my brothers and sisters, even if they are a pain in the neck.*
2. *If I see a new person at school looking lost I usually go and help them.*
3. *If someone else does something better than I do I mind a lot.*
4. *When I have done something well I make sure others know about it.*
5. *Sometimes I'm a bit rude to teachers (but only the ones who deserve it).*
6. *I get my own way and do what I want most of the time.*
7. *I am in a bad mood more than once a week.*
8. *If someone spilt ink all over my favourite T-shirt I would forgive them.*
9. *I get quite upset if I see someone being bullied.*
10. *If my friends let me down then I think they are not worth having as friends.*

Love in action

Rephrasing love
5 mins

Read the broken down version of 1 Corinthians 13:4–7 together from the worksheet. If necessary point out that the love test was based on the points Paul made about love in the passage. Then go round the group re-placing each description of love in the passage with a concrete example. So, instead of 'Love is patient' the first person might say, 'Love doesn't get ratty when a friend is five minutes late.' The second person might say, 'Love looks after people who are lonely' instead of, 'Love is kind.' Go round the group like this taking it in turns to rephrase a 'Love is...' saying. There is room on the worksheet to write these translations.

Jesus joins me on a typical day

Imagine this
4 mins

Ask the group to close their eyes and think back to their last school day. If Jesus had been following them around what would he have thought about the way they treated other people both at school and at home? What kind of love rating would he have given them? Ask them to write Jesus' thoughts in the bubble on the worksheets. You might like to go on to discuss practical ways in which they can try and show love at school and at home. The next activity gives a suggestion.

Taking stock

The crunch
4 mins

Get the group to think of someone they know (perhaps at school) who is, for whatever reason, either lonely, unhappy or unpopular. Ask them to imagine how that person must feel when they wake up on a Monday morning and write these thoughts in the bubble on the worksheets. Then ask them to think if there is anything that they could do to make life a little more bearable for this person.

Into action

Praying together
4 mins

Pass the present from week five round the group and encourage each person to pray a prayer for the person they identified in the 'Taking stock' section. Suggest that they also ask God to give them the guts to actually start caring for them. Conclude by reminding them that Love Treatment really works!

Looking back

A review
5 mins

Conclude the course by asking the group what they think they will remember about *Getting to Grips with God* in seventy years time as they sit in their robot-run old people's home on the planet Mars. If appropriate, go round the group sharing these thoughts and let them know what you've particularly enjoyed about the course or learnt from it.

End of series quiz

Looking back
10 mins

Hold an end of series quiz on all that you have done in *Getting to Grips with God*. Think up two or three questions on each of the ten meetings and score using a giant noughts and crosses board marked out with masking tape on the floor. When one of the two teams correctly answers a question one of their team can position themselves on the board. If you have thirty questions you could have three games of human noughts and crosses.

Answers to tricky questions

There are a number of commonly asked questions that are not directly covered by *Getting to Grips with God*. Sample answers to ten such questions are given on the next few pages. Please use and adapt them as appropriate. They are as follows:

The *Getting to Grips with God* meetings deal with many of the key questions about the Christian faith. Below is a list of the questions covered. If any of these questions are put in the questions box it might be best to deal with them during the appropriate meeting or remind them of what was said in that meeting.

1. Why does God let people suffer?

How can a loving, powerful God allow suffering in his world? What is God playing at? Is he asleep or does he not care? Unfortunately, this question is impossible to answer conclusively (God alone knows what he is playing at), but here are some clues to shed light on this most difficult of issues.

Self-inflicted
The Bible tells us that suffering is not part of God's original plan for life on earth and it will have no place in heaven (Revelation 21:4). It entered human experience when we decided to ignore God and run things our way. Most suffering therefore is the direct result of human behaviour. For example:

- Some suffering is the result of our own stupidity. E.g. if you ignore the 'Danger—slippery floor' sign, fall over and break your arm, you've got no one to blame but yourself.

- Most suffering is the direct result of someone else's sin. E.g. those who suffer any kind of abuse do so because of the decisions of their abuser.

- Larger scale suffering is also often caused by the sin of others. E.g. a department store in Seoul collapsed killing hundreds. The disaster was allegedly caused by the management ignoring warnings from staff the day before that the building was cracking up.

- Even global suffering can be the result of human behaviour. E.g. the suffering experienced during famines is often caused by war or bad government and even so could be avoided if the world's resources were fairly shared.

God uses suffering
This sounds a bit crazy I know, but think of it like this. If you accidentally touch something hot, you immediately feel the heat and before you know what you're doing you've pulled your hand away. The pain caused by the heat, saved you from getting very badly burnt. Suffering is never good in itself, but God does use it to make us into more caring, understanding, mature people. (The most convincing way to get this point across is to give a personal example of God changing you through suffering, or tell the group about the experience of a friend. For example, ever since she was a child, Jane has suffered from psoriasis, an unpleasant eczema-like skin condition. Through that daily experience she has learnt not to judge other people by their appearance and that God is more interested in what we are like inside than out.)

God's been there before
This is the most important point. We may resent the fact that God permits suffering in the world, but we must remember that he has suffered as much as any of us. In the person of Jesus, God has been through suffering and understands what it is like completely. The story of The Long Silence (opposite) makes the point well. Read it to the group.

Something to look forward to
Though many people go through the most appalling suffering here and now, God has a much better future planned for all who love him. In heaven, God will wipe out evil and suffering once and for all. It is easy to forget that there is more to our lives than just our time on planet earth. There is eternal paradise with God to come. As C.S. Lewis put it 'our life in this world is only the cover and the title page: when we die we begin Chapter One of the Great Story which no one on earth has read: which goes on forever: in which every chapter is better than the one before.'[7]

See also the answer to the question 'Where does evil come from?' on page 119.

The Long Silence

At the end of time, billions of people were scattered on the great plain before God's throne.

Most shrank back from the brilliant light before them, but some groups near the front talked heatedly—not with cringing shame, but with belligerence. 'Can God judge us? How can he know about suffering?' snapped a young brunette. She ripped open a sleeve to reveal a tattooed number from a Nazi concentration camp. 'We endured… terror… beatings… torture… death!'

In another group a young man lowered his collar. 'What about this?' he demanded, showing an ugly rope burn. 'Lynched… for no crime but being black!'

In another crowd, a pregnant school girl with sullen eyes. 'Why should I suffer?' she murmured. 'It wasn't my fault.'

Far out across the plain there were hundreds of such groups. Each had a complaint against God for the evil and suffering he permitted in his world. How lucky God was to live in heaven where all was sweetness and light, where there was no weeping or fear, no hunger or hatred. What did God know of all that man had been forced to endure in this world? For God leads a pretty sheltered life, they said.

So each of these groups sent forth their leader, chosen because he had suffered the most. A Jew, a young black man, a person from Hiroshima, a horribly deformed arthritic, a thalidomide child. In the centre of the plain they consulted with each other. At last they were ready to present their case. It was rather clever.

Before God could be qualified to be their judge, he must endure what they had endured. Their decision was that God should be sentenced to live on earth—as a man!

'Let him be born a Jew. Let the legitimacy of his birth be doubted. Give him a work so difficult that even his family will think him out of his mind when he tries to do it. Let him be betrayed by his closest friends. Let him face false charges, be tried by a prejudiced jury and convicted by a cowardly judge. Let him be tortured.

'At the last, let him see what it means to be terribly alone. Then let him die. Let him die so that there can be no doubt that he died. Let there be a whole host of witnesses to verify it.'

As each leader announced his portion of the sentence, loud murmurs of approval went up from the throng of people assembled.

And when the last had finished pronouncing sentence, there was a long silence. No one uttered another word. No one moved. For suddenly all knew that God had already served his sentence.

2. What happens when we die?

Trying to explain what happens after we die is rather like a dog trying to explain to another dog what it's like to be human. However, the Bible does tell us a bit about what happens after death.

- Death is not the end. We humans are created 'to be like God' and so we will live forever.

- Every human being will be judged by God. The basis of this judgment will be a person's response to God and it will be absolutely fair.

- God won't force himself on people who didn't want anything to do with him on earth. The Bible talks about 'hell' and it's a serious matter.

- People who have accepted God's offer of forgiveness through Jesus will be welcomed into his kingdom where they will share a wonderful, perfect and never-ending life with God (gasp) and all the members of his family (can't wait).

- In heaven we will not need our earthly bodies any more. These wear out as we live our life on earth (rather like an old suit of clothes), and one day will finally pack up and die. In heaven we will be transformed and kitted out in a new, heavenly body. The story of the 'Water Bugs and the Dragonflies' illustrates this transformation. Briefly it goes like this:

Deep below the surface of a pond lived a colony of water bugs. Occasionally one of their number would start crawling up the stalk of a lily pad and disappear for ever. This always confused and upset the water bugs, so one of them decided that when the time came for him to start climbing the lily stalk he would come back and tell the rest what happened. Not so many days later this very bug started climbing. He broke through the water into the warm sun and immediately fell asleep on the lily pad. When he woke up, he stretched and was amazed to find that he had turned into a dragonfly. With delight he soared into the air on his sparkling new wings. As he flitted here and there he looked down and saw his old friends below the surface of the pond and remembered his promise. Immediately he darted down, but only bounced off the surface of the pond. He tried again but soon realised to his dismay that he couldn't go back. 'Oh well,' he thought 'they wouldn't have recognised me in my new body. They will just have to wait until they become dragonflies too and then they will understand.' So he flew off to enjoy his new world of sun and air.[8]

3. Doesn't science disprove the Bible?

A lot of people think that science has disproved the Bible. They think that the theory of evolution contradicts God's account of the creation of the world in Genesis chapter one. This is most definitely not the case. They actually complement each other very well. Science tells us the '**how**' of the world—**how** the world came about. The Bible doesn't attempt to explain that, but focuses on '**why**' the world was made and **why** we are alive.

To demonstrate this boil a kettle in front of the group. Explain that a scientist would say that the kettle is boiling because the electric filament is heating the water to a temperature of 100 ºC and causing it to vaporize. You, on the other hand, might say that the kettle is boiling because you switched it on to make a cup of tea. Ask the group which they think is the truth. They are of course both true. It is the same with science and the Bible. The Bible tells us the 'why' of human existence, whereas science deals with the nuts and bolts of how we exist. They are both true—they just answer different questions.

4. What about other religions?

Human beings have an in-built need to be friends with God and that is why there is such a large number of different religions in the world. The crucial question is, 'Are all religions right?' Logically they can't be because they disagree with each other in important ways. Christians believe that Jesus was God, but Muslims believe that he was not God—only a good prophet. They can't both be right. The Bible tells us that the only way we can be friends with God is if we accept God's forgiveness through the death of Jesus. Other religions disagree.

In the end we can be sure of two things:

- If we ask God to forgive us for our sin and be 'in charge' of our life he will, and we can be his friends for ever.

- There are many people of other religions who, like us, say that they love and worship God, and it is not our business to criticize them. God is the only person who can justly judge human beings and we can be certain that he is fair and merciful and will always do the right thing.

5. Who made God?

Take a piece of string and lay it out on the floor. Explain to the group that it represents time. Time flows in only one direction from one end of the string (the beginning of time) to the other (the end of time). We humans are somewhere in between and we can only head in one direction. You can't decide to hop back in time and visit your great-grandparents. God, on the other hand, is outside time. He is not trapped in time like us humans. He is all around the string (like the carpet or floor). He can see all the string at once. As God is outside the confines of time there is no before or after with God. He is just there. So the question of who made God is not really an issue.

6. Where does evil come from?

The Bible does not explain the origins of evil and treats it as a bit of a mystery, but it does make the following points:

- God is opposed to evil, it was not part of his original design for his world, and he will not let it go on for ever. One day he is going to stamp it out once and for all. In heaven there will be no more death, no more grief or crying or pain (Revelation 21:4).
- Human beings are responsible for the evil in the world. God gave human beings the freedom to choose how they behave and, more importantly, to choose whether to love him or not. (If God had forced us to love and obey him our love for him would not be love. If you forced someone to marry you against their will and gave them a drug to make them love you, your relationship would be meaningless. Love is only love when it is freely given.) God gave us the freedom to choose whether to love him. When we decided to turn God down and do things our way, a 'way in' for evil was created. If we had all loved and obeyed God there would be no evil in the world. Evil is the inevitable result of some of the choices we humans have made.
- God will not stop evil now because if he were to do so it would mean that he would be removing our ability to choose how to behave. We would then be drugged-up robots and not humans at all.

7. How do I know if I am a Christian?

Sometimes people worry that they don't **feel** like a Christian any more. Does that mean that they are no longer a Christian or perhaps never were one? In week five we saw that a Christian is someone who has realised that they are not very good at running their own life in the way God wants and has asked Jesus to be 'in charge'. If you have done that at some point in the past you **are** a Christian even if you don't feel any different, even if you don't understand everything about God and even if you don't always obey your new boss. Here are two points to note:

- For some people becoming a Christian is a dramatic and emotional experience, but for others (like myself) nothing much seems to happen. This is because God treats us as individuals and works in our lives in different ways depending on what is best for us. So don't worry about why your experience of becoming or being a Christian is different from someone else's. It is just as real; the only difference is that God's dealings with you are made to fit your measurements, not anyone else's.

- Always try and remember that your relationship with God is based on facts not feelings. The facts of the Christian faith are that God loves you, Jesus has died for you, and the Holy Spirit is living in you. Just because you have a rotten day and feel terrible doesn't mean God has abandoned you. Christians will go through all sorts of experiences, good and bad and their feelings will change appropriately. Feelings are part of being human. The good news is that no matter what our feelings, nothing can separate us from God's love. (See Romans 8:38–39)

8. Why doesn't God DO something?

Why doesn't God DO something to make people believe in him?

'If God would only make himself visible,' the theory goes, 'if he would write his name across the sky in clouds or send a broadcast to planet earth from outer space, then everyone would believe in him.' Or would they? I think it is very unlikely for two reasons.

- God made himself visible in the person of Jesus 2,000 years ago, and did everyone believe in him? No way! In fact, they killed him. No doubt history would repeat itself.
- Some people once asked Jesus for a miracle (as if they hadn't had enough already) so that they could know that God was behind him. Jesus replied that the only miracle they would get would be to see him killed and alive again three days later. Sadly that wasn't good enough for them. But the death and resurrection of Jesus really are God's ultimate act. God *has* done something! And that something has changed human lives more than any other single event in the history of our planet.

Why doesn't God DO something about the mess the world is in?

I remember once seeing a cartoon that answered this question rather well. Two people were sitting under a tree. One says to the other, 'I was going to ask God why he doesn't do something about the mess the world is in.' 'Why didn't you?' came the reply. 'Because I thought he might ask me the same question.'

God has done and is doing a great deal about the mess the world is in. But he has chosen to use human beings as his main agents for doing his business on earth. We need to go one step further than the cartoon and ask God what he wants US to do about the mess the world is in.

See also the answer to the question, 'Where does evil come from?' on page 119.

9. How can I help my friends meet God?

It is good and natural to want your friends and family to meet God. So how can you help them and what should you do if they are not interested? Well, you can't force anyone to be interested in God, but you can make a difference. Here are three ways you can do that:

- Try and follow Jesus' instructions in the way you live your life. Seeing the difference that God makes to you will have a big impact on your friends and family (even if they don't admit it). They will be watching you, seeing how you behave, and figuring out in their minds whether you have got something that is worth having. Even if they are not interested in finding out about God, they will begin to see what he is like by looking at you. You are God's walking advertisement. That sounds quite a responsibility, but God is at work in us, making us like himself. He doesn't expect us to become perfect overnight, but just to keep trying to follow him and make a bit of progress each day.
- Be ready to help your friends when they have needs. Practical caring is very powerful.
- Pray for them. Pray that God will help them to realize that he loves them and that they need him.

This may take a very long time, even ten, twenty, thirty years, but if you do these three things then God will be at work in the lives of your friends and family and will use you to introduce him to them.

10. Do pets go to heaven?

The honest answer is that we don't really know. Our knowledge of heaven is very sketchy. It is about as complete as what you can know about a castle or palace from a rough sketch or photo. (Perhaps you could show the group a sketch of your home or church building.) The drawing may give you a feel of the place but certainly no idea of what wonders are to be found inside or even round the back. We will have to wait till we get there to find out the awesome reality behind our sketchy ideas of heaven. Bearing that in mind we can make three points about pets in heaven.

- The first is that God made all the animals in the world and he was very pleased with his handiwork. Animals are part of God's wonderful creation and there is no real reason to believe that God would exclude them from his final perfect kingdom.

- Secondly, in the Old Testament, a prophet named Isaiah gives us a picture of how things will be when God finally establishes his kingdom (Isaiah 11:1–9). He describes wolves and sheep living together in peace, leopards lying down with young goats, calves and lion cubs feeding together, and little children taking care of them. Though we should not take this too literally, it does give us a picture of animals in heaven. And what is more, animals in heaven getting on well with each other and human beings!

- The third point is that we there will be no sadness in heaven. Whether our pets are there or not somehow we will all be overflowing with God's happiness. Life with God will be infinitely more wonderful than life now, pets or no pets. But let's hope that they get to share it with us!

Useful information

Getting to Grips with God audio cassette

The *Getting to Grips with God* audio cassette contains all the *Getting to Grips with God* sound effects and theme tunes and is available from your local Christian bookshop or, in case of difficulty, direct from BRF. See page 143 for details.

Books to help you answer tough questions

The Superglue Sandwich, David Lawrence, Scripture Union, 1993
An excellent book answering nine questions about the Christian faith. Ideal for young people and not bad for leaders either.

If I Could Ask God One Question, Greg Johnson, Tyndale, 1991
Good clear answers to roughly 100 tough questions about the Christian faith for young Christians.

The Questions Children Ask, Penny Frank, CPAS, 1994
One hundred answers parents need about God and the world we live in. The answers are aimed at slightly younger children, but this is probably the best book to help you answer your group's questions.

Answers to Tough Questions, Josh McDowell, Scripture Press, 1980
A book of brief answers for adults to many questions about the Christian faith.

Handbook of Christian Apologetics, Kreeft & Tacelli, IVP, 1994
Hundreds of clear and concise answers to key questions. A useful reference book to have on your bookshelves. It will help you figure out answers to tough questions though you will need to adapt them for young people.

Know the Truth, Bruce Milne, IVP, 1982
A handbook of the Christian faith. If you're not quite sure about any Christian doctrine here's the book to help you get it sorted out.

References

1. **All God's Children**, General Synod Board of Education and Mission, 1991
2. C.S. Lewis, **The Abolition of Man**, Fount, 1943
3. Shakespeare, **Hamlet**, II. ii. 316
4. Frederic Kenyon, **The Bible and Archaeology**
5. Mother Teresa of Calcutta, **A Gift for God**, Collins Fount Paperbacks, 1981
6. Mother Teresa of Calcutta, **A Gift for God**, Collins Fount Paperbacks, 1981
7. C.S. Lewis, **The Last Battle**, Pengin, 1956
8. Doris Stickney, **Waterbugs and Dragonflies**, Mowbray, 1982

Hello, my name's GOD, I don't think you know me.

No, I'm not sure I do...

Meeting One

Getting to Grips *with God*

In our first Getting to Grips with God meeting we will be investigating GOD and grappling with such questions as:

● What's God like?
● What's he do all day?
● Where is he?
● Who is he?
● How do we know he exists at all?

Taking stock

What has really struck you in this meeting?

....

If you could ask God one question and get a straight answer what would you ask?

....

Has your notion of God changed during this meeting?

Yes ☐   No ☐   Not sure ☐

If so, how? ....

QUOTE OF THE WEEK

'God comes to meet those who search for him.'

Anonymous

God is...

In the space below write all the God words that you can remember from the 'God is...' word game.

God is . . .

Getting to know you

Pair up with another member of the group and find out the following facts.

Name

Last thing eaten

Pet details

Favourite colour

Most enjoyable experience

Self portrait in three words

Ambitions

Invent a God

If you were to invent God what would he, she or it be like? Jot down your thoughts on the clipboard below.

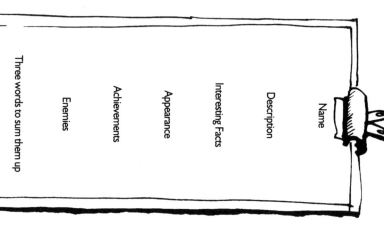

Name

Description

Interesting Facts

Appearance

Achievements

Enemies

Three words to sum them up

When I think of God…

Jot down the first things that come into your head when you think of God. Don't worry if they're strange!

Ponder this

Ever since God created the world, his invisible qualities, both his eternal power and his divine nature, have been clearly seen; they are perceived in the things that God has made. So people have no excuse at all!

Romans I verse 20

Natural evidence

What do you remember about the mind-boggling, multi-sensory experience? Jot it all down here.

Meeting Two

Getting to Grips with Life

In our second Getting to Grips with God meeting we will be looking at LIFE and grappling with such thorny questions as:

- Why am I alive?
- What's the meaning of life?
- What makes a human human?
- What's God got to do with it?
- Why is the world in such a mess?

Taking stock

What have you discovered about the meaning of life?

....

....

What's gone wrong with the human race?

....

....

QUOTE OF THE WEEK

God created human beings, making them to be like himself.

Genesis 1 verse 27

In God's shoes

So what should God do about the fact that we human beings so often choose to do what's wrong? What should he do about the fact that his children so often don't give a damn about him? Write your suggestions on this postcard.

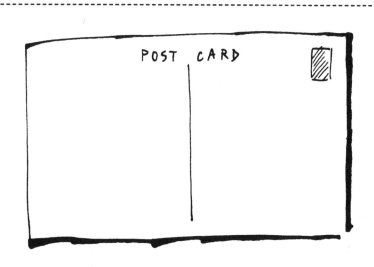

POST CARD

Why are we alive?

Then God said,

"And now we will make human beings; they will be like us and resemble us. They will have power over the fish, the birds, and all animals, domestic and wild, large and small."

So God created human beings, making them to be like himself... God looked at everything he had made, and he was very pleased.

Genesis 1 verses 26–31

What does this poem from the beginning of the Bible tell you about why we are alive? Jot your thoughts down here.

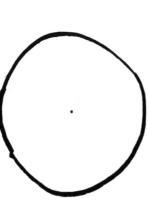

What would you do?

Tick the boxes on the left to show what you **would** do in each of these ten situations? Then tick the boxes on the right to show what you **should** do in each.

What would you do?   **What should you do?**

yes no   yes no

You find a wallet containing £20. Would you keep the dosh?

You drop your new personal stereo and break it. There is no visible damage. Would you try and claim the repairs under the guarantee?

A good friend has become famous. A journalist offers you loads of money for juicy info about their past. Would you take it and tell all?

On a cold winter's day you see an old lady slip over on the pavement. Would you try to help?

One of your friends makes a racist remark. Would you say anything?

You have been invited to the party of a life time. You cant find a babysitter for your 6 & 8 yr. old kids. Do you leave them by themselves?

You hear that your form tutor has started going out with the head's daughter/son. Would you pass it round the class?

At school you see your best mate being beaten up. Would you try to help?

You've had a bad day. When you get home your Mum says something harmless which you find very annoying. Would you get ratty?

You were on your way to spend a fiver on the lottery when you see a person collecting for famine relief. Would you give the £5 to feed the hungry?

In how many of the ten questions did you tick two 'yes' or two 'no' boxes. Write your score here. If your score is near nought then there is a big gap between what you know you should do and what you actually do. The nearer you are to ten the better you are a doing what you know you should. Well done.

What's gone wrong?

Imagine that someone has got your whole life on video. How much of it would you be happy to have screened on prime time TV, how much would you pay megga bucks not to have screened, and how much would you not be bothered about? Fill in the pie chart with these proportions.

The point is that we often don't do what we know we should. The Bible puts it like this:

'Everyone has sinned and is far away from God's saving presence.
Romans 3 verse 23

THE BIG IMPACT

Meeting Three

Getting to Grips with Jesus

In our third Getting to Grips with God meeting we are going to be investigating JESUS, and grappling with such questions as:

- What's the big deal about Jesus?
- What did he do?
- Was he mad, bad or God?
- Why are we still talking about him today?
- What's he got to do with me?

Taking stock

Martha said that Jesus was the Son of God. Jesus also make that claim for himself and there are only three ways of explaining it. Tick which ever seems the best explanation?

☐ He was a liar

☐ He was mad

☐ He was telling the truth

Why do you think people are still following Jesus 2,000 years on?

....

....

Has anything particularly struck you in this meeting? What is it and why?

....

....

QUOTE OF THE WEEK

Jesus Christ is no one less than the invisible God made visible.

Colossians 1 verse 15

Discoveries

Note down the five important things that these events underline (clue) about Jesus.

1. ....

2. ....

3. ....

4. ....

5. ....

Now turn these into punchy newspaper headlines

1. ....

2. ....

3. ....

4. ....

5. ....

ECHO

Match 'n' mix

If you matched 'n mixed your favourite person or hero with your partner's hero, who would you get and what would they be like! Fill in your results here.

Match 'n' Mix	
.... &	
Name	
Age	
Character	
Favourite expression	
Hobbies	
Profession	
Fashion style	
Favourite pop group	
Ultimate Ambitions	

God 'n' man

If you matched 'n' mixed God and a human being what would you get? Fill in your thoughts.

Match 'n' Mix God + a human	
Name	
Age	
Character	
Favourite expression	
Hobbies	
Profession	
Fashion style	
Favourite pop group	
Ultimate Ambitions	

A telling incident

In this telling incident from God's life on earth, Jesus has come to visit his friends Mary and Martha whose brother has just died.

Narrator: When Jesus arrived, he found that Lazarus had been buried four days before. When Martha heard that Jesus was coming, she went out to meet him.

Martha: If you had been here, Lord, my brother would not have died! But I know that even now God will give you whatever you ask him for.

Jesus: Your brother will rise to life.

Martha: I know that he will rise to life on the last day.

Jesus: I am the resurrection and the life. Those who believe in me will live, even though they die; and all those who live and believe in me will never die. Do you believe this?

Martha: Yes, Lord! I do believe that you are the Messiah, the Son of God, who was to come into the world.

Narrator: When Jesus saw her weeping, and saw how the people who were with her were weeping also, his heart was touched, and he was deeply moved.

Jesus: Where have you buried him?

Person 1: Come and see, Lord.

Narrator: Jesus wept.

Person 1: See how much he loved him!

Person 2: He gave sight to the blind man, didn't he? Could he not have kept Lazarus from dying?

Narrator: Deeply moved once more, Jesus went to the tomb, which was a cave with a stone placed at the entrance.

Jesus: Take the stone away!

Martha: There will be a bad smell, Lord. He has been buried four days!

Jesus: Didn't I tell you that you would see God's glory if you believed?

Narrator: They took the stone away, Jesus looked up to heaven.

Jesus: I thank you, Father, that you listen to me. I know that you always listen to me, but I say this for the sake of the people here, so that they will believe that you sent me. (loud) Lazarus, come out!

Narrator: He came out, his hands and feet wrapped in grave clothes, and with a cloth round his face.

Jesus: Untie him and let him go.

Narrator: Many of the people who had come to visit Mary and Martha saw what Jesus did and they believed in him.

Shocking! I don't know why God doesn't do something about the mess we're all in!

JESUS MURDERED

Meeting Four

Getting to Grips with the Rescue

In our fourth Getting to Grips with God meeting we are going to be investigating GOD'S RESCUE PLAN FOR THE HUMAN RACE and grappling with such questions as:

- Why was Jesus nailed?
- What's it got to do with me?
- Who nicked the body?
- Did Jesus rise again?
- If so, where's the evidence?

The Resurrection

Jot down some words that describe your reaction to the resurrection of Jesus.

PS When God raised Jesus from the dead he showed that he accepted Jesus' death in our place. Because of the resurrection we can know that God's rescue plan for our rescue has worked. Huuraaay!

QUOTE OF THE WEEK

Because of our sins Jesus was handed over to die, and he was raised to life in order to put us right with God.

Romans 4:25

The illustrations

Which of the following illustrations most helped you to understand why Jesus died? (Ring one.)

Taking stock

Put a cross somewhere on each line to indicate how much you agree or disagree with each statement

1. Jesus was a great teacher but not the Son of God.

strongly agree _____ strongly disagree

2. Jesus' death was a tragic mistake.

strongly agree _____ strongly disagree

3. Jesus' death was something to do with me.

strongly agree _____ strongly disagree

4. When Jesus died he was taking the punishment for my sin.

strongly agree _____ strongly disagree

The death of Jesus

Pilate: Jesus stood before the Roman governor, who questioned him. *"Are you the king of the jews?"*

Jesus: *"So you say,"* answered Jesus.

Pilate: But he said nothing in response to the accusations of the chief priests and elders. So Pilate said to him, *"Don't you hear all these things they accuse you of?"* But Jesus refused to answer a single word, with the result that the Governor was greatly surprised.

At every Passover Festival the Roman governor was in the habit of setting free any one prisoner the crowd asked for. At that time there was a well-known prisoner named Barabbas. So when the crowd gathered, Pilate asked them, *"Which one do you want me to set free for you? Barabbas or Jesus called the Messiah?"* He knew very well that the Jewish authorities had handed Jesus over to him because they were jealous.

Pilate's wife: While Pilate was sitting in the judgement hall, his wife sent him a message: *"Have nothing to do with that innocent man, because in a dream last night I suffered much on account of him."*

Chief Priest: The chief priests and the elders persuaded the crowd to ask Pilate to set Barabbas free and have Jesus put to death.

Pilate: But Pilate asked the crowd, *"Which one of these two do you want me to set free for you?"*

Crowd: *"BARABBAS!"*

Pilate: *"What, then, shall I do with jesus called the Messiah?"*

Crowd: *"CRUCIFY HIM!"*

Pilate: *"What crime has he committed?"*

Crowd: Then they started shouting at the top of their voices: *"CRUCIFY HIM!"*

Pilate: When Pilate saw that it was no use to go on, but that a riot might break out, he took some water, washed his hands in front of the crowd, and said, *"I am not responsible for the death of this man! This is your doing!"*

Crowd: The whole crowd answered, *"Let the responsibility for his death fall on us and our children!"*

Barabbas: Then Pilate set Barabbas free for them; and after he had Jesus whipped, he handed him over to be crucified.

Roman soldier: Then Pilate's soldiers took Jesus into the governor's palace, and the whole company gathered round him. They stripped off his clothes and put a scarlet robe on him. Then they made a crown out of thorny branches and placed it on his head, and put a stick in his right hand; then they knelt before him and mocked him. *"LONG LIVE THE KING OF THE JEWS!"* they said. They spat on him, and took the stick and hit him over the head. When they had finished mocking him, they took the robe off and put his own clothes back on him. Then they led him out to crucify him.

Simon: As they were going out, they met a man from Cyrene named Simon, and the soldiers forced him to carry Jesus' cross. They came to a place called Golgotha, which means, *"The Place of the Skull."* There they offered Jesus wine mixed with a bitter substance; but after tasting it, he would not drink it.

Roman Soldier: They crucified him and then divided his clothes among them by throwing dice. After that they sat there and watched him. Above his head they put the written notice of the accusation against him: *"This is Jesus, the King of the Jews."* Then they crucified two bandits with Jesus, one on his right and the other on his left.

Passers by: People passing by shook their heads and hurled insults at Jesus: *"You were going to tear down the Temple and build it up again in three days! Save yourself if you are God's Son! Come on down from the cross!"*

Chief priests: In the same way the chief priests and the teachers of the Law and the elders jeered at him: *"He saved others, but he cannot save himself! Isn't he the king of Israel? If he comes down off the cross now, we will believe in him! He trusts in God and claims to be God's Son. Well, then, let us see if God wants to save him now!"*

Thief: Even the bandits who had been crucified with him insulted him in the same way.

Jesus: At noon the whole country was covered with darkness, which lasted for three hours. At about three o'clock Jesus cried out with a loud shout, *"My God, my God, why did you abandon me?"*

Passers by: Some of the people standing there heard him and said, *"He is calling for Elijah!"* One of them ran up at once, took a sponge, soaked it in cheap wine, put it on the end of a stick, and tried to make him drink it. But the others said, *"Wait, let us see if Elijah is coming to save him!"* Jesus again gave a loud cry and breathed his last.

Army Officer: Then the curtain hanging in the Temple was torn in two from top to bottom. The earth shook, the rocks split apart, the graves broke open, and many of God's people who had died were raised to life. They left the graves, and after Jesus rose from death, they went into the Holy City, where many people saw them. When the army officer and the soldiers with him who were watching Jesus saw the earthquake and everything else that happened, they were terrified and said, *"He really was the Son of God!"*

Ponder this

What does the death of Jesus mean to you?

....

....

What would you like to ask Jesus about his death?

....

....

Meeting Five

Getting to Grips with Becoming a Christian

In our fifth Getting to Grips with God meeting we are going to be investigating BECOMING A CHRISTIAN and grappling with such questions as:

- How do I become a Christian?
- How do I know if I'm one already?
- How do I know if I'm ready?
- What will it cost?
- And what will happen next?

Pros & cons

Make a list of the pros and cons of becoming a Christian. How do they weigh up?

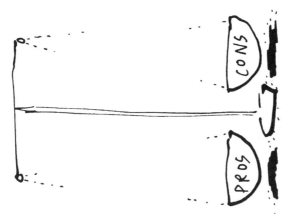

Taking stock

What has been the crunch in this meeting for you?
....

What will you do about it?....................................
....

My question list

Make a list of all the questions you have about the Christian faith. Why not keep this list and tick off the questions as and when you get good answers.

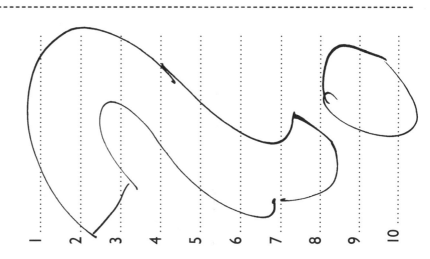

1 ....
2 ....
3 ....
4 ....
5 ....
6 ....
7 ....
8 ....
9 ....
10 ....

What is a Christian?

- A Christian is someone who has realized that they are not very good at being 'in charge' of their life. They are sorry that they haven't been living in a way that pleases God and have asked him to forgive them.

- A Christian is someone who has asked God to be 'in charge' of their life. Imagine your life is a football or netball team. When you were the captain things weren't too hot; you won the odd game but lost many more and got quite a few red and yellow cards for bad behaviour. Now there is a new captain in charge' he wants changes made; harder training, new game plan, total loyalty. It's like that with God; once he is 'in charge' of your life he'll need to start making changes too so that you start living in a way that pleases God.

Is all this crystal clear, or is there anything that you don't quite understand or would like to ask?

Where do you stand?

Read through the five positions and tick the one that best describes how you feel.

1. ☐ I know I'm not good at running my life and have asked God to be 'in charge'. I'm not perfect and don't understand it all, but I am a Christian.

2. ☐ I'm not sure if I've asked God to be in charge of my life or not. I don't know if I'm a Christian.

3. ☐ I think I understand what becoming a Christian would mean but I'm not ready to ask God to be 'in charge' of my life just yet.

4. ☐ This is all a bit confusing and I don't really know what to think.

5. ☐ I realize that I'm not good at running my life in a way that pleases God. I'm really sorry about this and would like to ask God to be 'in charge' of my life from now on.

What should I do?

Please chat to any of the Getting to Grips with God leaders about where you stand. If you have ticked box five and want to accept Jesus' free gift and ask him to be 'in charge' of your life all you need to do is tell him. Tell him that you are sorry for making a mess of running your life and that you would like him to be 'in charge' from now on. He'll be delighted and you will have joined his family. Well done!

As a start why not tell a Christian friend that you have decided to follow Jesus. Jot their name down here.

Thank you God

Why not write a prayer to God thanking him for his wonderful free gift of forgiveness and love?

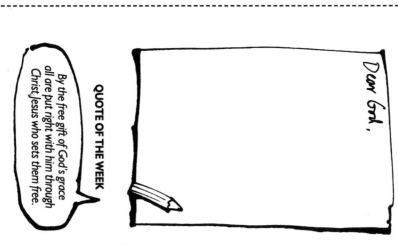

Dear God,

QUOTE OF THE WEEK

By the free gift of God's grace all are put right with him through Christ Jesus who sets them free.

GOOD TO SEE
YOU JO.
HOW ARE YOU?

How long have
you got?

Meeting Six

Getting to Grips
with Prayer

In our sixth Getting to Grips with God meeting we are going to be investigating PRAYER and grappling with such questions as:

- *Can I really talk to God?*
- *Will he talk to me?*
- *How should I do it?*
- *Where should I do it?*
- *How do I know if he's listening?*

Taking stock

What has struck you most in this meeting?

....
....

Make a prayer 'plan of attack' for the week ahead. Decide on one way in which you can pray a bit more in the week ahead and write it here.

QUOTE OF THE WEEK

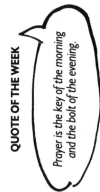

*Prayer is the key of the morning
and the bolt of the evening.*

Matthew Henry

Pictured prayers

Choose a photo from a magazine of something that interests you and turn it into a prayer. If there is no room on the photo use this space to write your prayer.

smile!

Prayer is…

How would you complete the sentence 'Prayer is…?'
Jot your thoughts down here.

Jot down anything that struck you in the Lord's
Prayer sketch.

Jesus on prayer

Jesus said to his disciples: 'When you pray, go to your
room, close the door, and pray to your Father, who is
unseen. And your Father, who sees what you do in
private, will reward you. When you pray, do not use a lot
of meaningless words, as the pagans do, who think that
their gods will hear them because their prayers are long.
Do not be like them. Your Father already knows what
you need before you ask him.

This, then, is how you should pray:

- Our Father in heaven: May your holy name be
  honoured;

- may your Kingdom come; may your will be done on
  earth as it is in heaven.

- Give us today the food we need.

- Forgive us the wrongs we have done, as we forgive
  the wrongs that others have done to us.

- Do not bring us to hard testing, but keep us safe
  from the Evil One.

If you forgive others the wrongs they have done to you,
your Father in heaven will also forgive you. But if you do
not forgive others, then your Father will not forgive the
wrongs you have done.   Matthew 6 verses 5–15

The handy hints

Try and draw or list all ten prayer objects and next to
each jot down the prayer hints they give us.

Meeting Seven

Getting to Grips with the Bible

This'll be that letter from God I've been waiting for!

In our seventh Getting to Grips with God meeting we are going to be taking a look into THE BIBLE and grappling with such questions as:

● What's the Bible all about?
● Who wrote it and where did it come from?
● Why should I read it?
● Where do I start?
● And what will it do for me?

Taking stock

Has you attitude to the Bible changed in this meeting?

Yes ☐   No ☐   Not sure ☐

If so how? ....

How might this affect your life? ....

QUOTE OF THE WEEK

It ain't those parts of the Bible that I can't understand that bother me, it is the parts I do understand.

Mark Twain

Handy hints

Here are five tips on how to go about reading the Bible with Lightning Bolts daily Bible readings.

● Try and find a quiet place and a regular time (5 mins).

● Ask God to help you understand what you read.

● Read the Bible passage and the comment on it.

● Do the activity or answer the questions. These will help you understand what the passage is all about.

● Ponder or pray about what the passage has to say.

First impressions

Jot down the very first thoughts that come into your head when you think of the Bible.

Pass the parcel

Jot down everything you can remember about the Bible from the pass the parcel.

Life manual

43

Read: 2 Timothy 3 verse 16

All Scripture [the Bible] is inspired by God and is useful for teaching the truth, rebuking error, correcting faults, and giving instruction for right living, so that the person who serves God may be fully qualified and equipped to do every kind of good deed.

Instruction manuals are jolly handy. I've got one that tells me how to use the computer package on which I'm writing this book. If I need to know how to use the 'Spell Check' for example, I can just look it up. Without the manual I'd spend ages messing around trying to work it out on my own.

In today's passage, Saint Paul tells us that the Bible is God's instruction manual for human life. Using the points he makes write a book review of the Bible for the magazine of your choice. (e.g. *Fashion Freaks* or *Body Builders' Weekly*)

Ponder this

If you are going to benefit from an instruction manual you have to actually read it. Over the last few weeks you have been reading extracts from the Bible in this book. So, your study of God's instruction manual is coming on well. Keep it up!

59

Prayer space

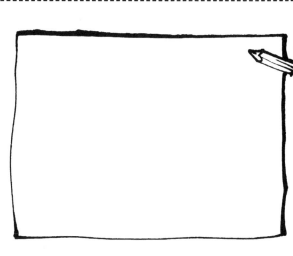

Wey hey! I surrender

THAT'S MY BOY

'S HOLY SPIRIT

Meeting Eight

Getting to Grips with the Holy Spirit

In our eighth Getting to Grips with God meeting we are going to be meeting THE HOLY SPIRIT and grappling with such questions as:

- Who is the Holy Spirit?
- How's he related to God?
- What's his line of business?
- How do I know if I've got him?
- What difference would it make if I had?

Taking stock

Do you want to become more like Jesus?

Yes ☐ No ☐ Not sure ☐

Are you ready to let the Holy Spirit start working on you?

Yes ☐ No ☐ Not sure ☐

Dear God...

Use this sheet of writing paper to write God a letter about the changes that you would like him to help you make in your life.

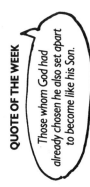

Becoming like Jesus

In the frame below make a list of words describing what you are like as a person. Include of your good and bad points and the other things that make you you.

In this frame make a list of words describing what God would like you to be like.

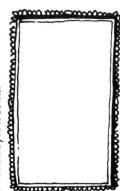

The job of the Holy Spirit is to help you become more like Jesus and your second set of words.

QUOTE OF THE WEEK

Those whom God had already chosen he also set apart to become like his Son.

Romans 8 verse 29

Imitators

- How much would you like to be like Jesus? Put a cross somewhere on the line between 'very much' and 'no thank you'.

very much ——————————— no thank you

- How hard would you find it to imitate him?

simple ——————————— impossible

- Where would you get it wrong most often?

....

The job of the Holy Spirit is to help us become more like Jesus as we shall soon see . . .

Becoming like Jesus

A TRAINING FILM FROM THE HOLY SPIRIT

Jesus on the Holy Spirit

Jesus said to his disciples,

'I will ask the Father, and he will give you another **Helper**, who will **stay with you for ever**. He is the Spirit who **reveals the truth about God**. The world cannot receive him, because it cannot see him or know him. But you know him, because he remains **with you and is in you**. The Helper, the Holy Spirit, whom the Father will send in my name, **will teach you everything** and **make you remember all that** I have told you.'

John 14 verses 16, 17 & 26

Holy Spirit fact file

Jot down the six jobs of the Holy Spirit mentioned by Jesus in the passage above.

1. ....
2. ....
3. ....
4. ....
5. ....
6. ....

Object lessons

Now jot down what the following objects tell us about the Holy Spirit.

Water, ice, steam

Egg

Battery

Jot down anything else you know about the Holy Spirit.

....
....
....

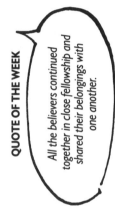

Meeting Nine

Getting to Grips with God's Family

In our ninth Getting to Grips with God meeting we will be thinking about GOD'S FAMILY and grappling with such questions as:

- Why does God have a family?
- Who is in his family?
- What happens at family parties?
- Does God's family need me?
- How can I be a good family member?

Taking stock

What have you discovered about being a member of God's family today?

....
....

What one thing could you do this week to support your brothers and sisters?

....
....

QUOTE OF THE WEEK

All the believers continued together in close fellowship and shared their belongings with one another.

Acts 2 verse 44

Process this

What does the food processor tell you about being part of God's family?

Meet the family

Go round the group and collect the signatures of people who fit these descriptions.

has more than two brothers or sisters
is a vegetarian
is the oldest child in their family
has a Mum who is under 34 years old
became a Christian this year
says they never argue with their parents
has a grandparent living in their house
has a baby brother or sister (under 2)
has a relative who is a twin
has more than ten letters in their surname

Family acts

Here is a passage from the Bible describing ten ways in which the first Christians treated each other like one big family.

They spent their time in learning from the apostles, taking part in fellowship, and sharing in the fellowship meals and the prayers. Many miracles and wonders were being done through the apostles, and everyone was filled with awe. All the believers continued together in close fellowship and shared their belongings with one another. They would sell their property and possessions, and distribute the money among all, according to what each one needed. Day after day they met as a group in the Temple, and they had their meals together in their homes, eating with glad and humble hearts, praising God, and enjoying the good will of all the people. And every day the Lord added to their group those who were being saved.

Acts 2 verses 42-47

Family act list

Make a list of the ten things these first Christians did together and for each other.

1. ....

2. ....

3. ....

4. ....

5. ....

6. ....

7. ....

8. ....

9. ....

10. ....

GOD'S GREAT
RECYCLING PLAN

Meeting Ten

Getting to Grips with Loving others

In our tenth and final Getting to Grips with God meeting we are going to be looking at LOVING OTHERS and grappling with such questions as:

- What does God want me to do for him?
- What's love got to do with it?
- Why is it so powerful?
- How do I love my neighbour?
- And who is my neighbour anyway?

Taking stock

Think of someone in your class who is the odd one out and gets a hard time from the rest. Make a list of words that describe how that person must feel when they wake up on a Monday morning.

What could you do to make their day more bearable?

Will you do it?   yes ☐   no ☐   might ☐

Why not write a prayer for them and while you're at it ask God to help you do something practical to help?

In seventy years time as you sit in your robot-run old people's home on the planet Mars what do you think you will remember about Getting to Grips with God?

Imagine this

Think back to your last day at school. If Jesus had been following you around what would he have thought about the way you treated other people both at school and at home? What kind of love rating would he have given you? Write his thoughts in the bubble here.

QUOTE OF THE WEEK

Now that you know how much God is in love with you, it is only natural that you spend the rest of your life radiating that love.

Mother Teresa

St Paul's Love Test

Answer the following questions as honestly as possible and find out how you fare on St Paul's love test.

yes no

1. I am patient with my brothers and sisters even if they are a pain in the neck. ☐ ☐

2. If I see a new person at school looking lost I usually go and help them. ☐ ☐

3. If someone else does something better than me I mind a lot. ☐ ☐

4. When I have done something well I make sure others know about it. ☐ ☐

5. Sometimes I'm a bit rude to teachers (but only the ones who deserve it). ☐ ☐

6. I get my own way and do what I want most of the time. ☐ ☐

7. I am in a bad mood more than once a week. ☐ ☐

8. If someone spilt ink all over my favourite T-shirt I wouldn't hold it against them. ☐ ☐

9. I get quite upset if I see someone being bullied. ☐ ☐

10. If my friends let me down then I think they are not worth having as friends. ☐ ☐

Love in action

Here are St Paul's thoughts on love taken from I Corinthians 13 verses 4–8. See if you can give examples of what each means in practice.

Love is patient ....

Love is kind ....

Love is not jealous ....

Love is not conceited ....

Love is not proud ....

Love is not ill-mannered ....

Love is not selfish ....

Love is not irritable ....

Love does not keep a record of wrongs ....

Love is not happy with evil ....

Love is happy with the truth ....

Love never gives up ....

Love's faith does not fail ....

Love's hope does not fail ....

Love's patience does not fail ....

Love is eternal ....

Getting to Grips with God Cassette

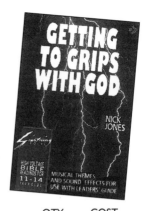

The *Getting to Grips with God* cassette contains all the sound effects and theme music you will need to run the *Getting to Grips with God* course. Available from your local Christian bookshop or, in case of difficulty, direct from BRF. Price £5.99.

PLEASE SEND ME THE FOLLOWING:

			QTY	COST
3088 3	Struck by Jesus (Leaders' Guide)	£5.99	_____	_____
3085 9	Struck by Jesus (Daily Notes)	£2.50	_____	_____
	Struck by Jesus (Daily Notes-10 pack)	£20.00	_____	_____
3276 2	Struck by Jesus (resource pack) (incl.VAT)	£5.99	_____	_____
3084 0	Out Of This World (Leaders' Guide)	£7.99	_____	_____
3083 2	Out Of This World (Daily Notes)	£2.99	_____	_____
	Out Of This World (Daily Notes-10 pack)	£25.00	_____	_____
3288 6	Out Of This World (audio cassette) (incl.VAT)	£5.99	_____	_____
3254 1	Getting To Grips With God (Leaders' Guide)	£8.99	_____	_____
3255 X	Getting To Grips With God (Daily Notes)	£2.99	_____	_____
	Getting To Grips With God (Daily Notes-10-pack)	£25.00	_____	_____
3527 3	**Getting To Grips With God (audio cassette)** (incl.VAT.)	£5.99	_____	_____
3259 2	Rise Up, Wise Up (Leaders' Guide)	£8.99	_____	_____
3260 6	Rise Up, Wise Up (Daily Notes)	£2.99	_____	_____
	Rise Up, Wise Up (Daily Notes-10-pack)	£25.00	_____	_____
3081 6	Rise Up, Wise Up (audio cassette) (incl.VAT.)	£5.99	_____	_____

Please complete the payment details below (all orders must be accompanied by the appropriate payment) and send your completed form to **BRF, Peter's Way, Sandy Lane West, Oxford OX4 5HG**.

Name . . . .

Address . . . .

. . . . Postcode . . . .

POSTAGE AND PACKING RATES

ORDER VALUE	UK	EUROPE	REST OF WORLD Surface	WORLD Airmail
£6.00 & under	£1.25	£2.25	£2.25	£3.50
£6.01-£14.99	£3.00	£3.50	£4.50	£6.00
£15.00-£29.99	£4.00	£5.50	£7.50	£11.00
£30.00 & over	free	enquire	enquire	enquire

Total value of books: £ _____

Postage and packing: £ _____

Donation to BRF: £ _____

Total enclosed: £ _____

Method of Payment: ☐ Cheque   ☐ Mastercard   ☐ Visa   ☐ Postal Order

Credit card number ☐☐☐☐ ☐☐☐☐ ☐☐☐☐ ☐☐☐☐

Expiry Date ☐☐☐☐

Signature _____   Date _____

The Bible Reading Fellowship, Peter's Way, Sandy Lane West, Oxford OX4 5HG
Tel: 01865 748227 Fax: 01865 773150 BRF is a registered charity (No. 233280)
Prices and postage rates valid until 31 December 1996

PLEASE KEEP ME INFORMED ABOUT BRF YOUNG PEOPLE'S RESOURCES ☐

The Lightning Bolts Series

Now that you have gone through *Getting to Grips with God*, you might like to know about other titles in the Lightning Bolts series. Following the same format as *Getting to Grips with God*, each course comprises a leaders' guide and daily notes, available from your local Christian bookshop or, in case of difficulty, direct from BRF.

Struck by Jesus

Takes ten incidents from Mark's Gospel and through them examines the extraordinary marks of God's life on earth; from his compassion to his authority, from his gentleness to his obedience.

Out of This World

Out of This World explores ten key themes in God's developing master-plan for the disaster-prone human race. Spanning from Genesis to Revelation it follows the epic history of God's relationship with human beings. The plan of the Master in the face of disaster is a heart-warming tale that is truly 'out of this world'.

Rise Up, Wise Up

Rise Up, Wise Up unpacks ten of the major themes from the book of Proverbs and will help you in your youth group take on board the wise sayings of yester-millennium and learn how to be wise today.

Close Encounters

By introducing you to ten diverse characters who close encounter Jesus in Luke's Gospel, *Close Encounters* will help you and your youth group to close encounter him yourselves.

Struck by Jesus and **Out of This World** are already published. **Rise Up, Wise Up** *will be available in summer 1996 and* **Close Encounters** *in the autumn of 1996. Please phone the BRF office to confirm prices.*